When I Am Weak

When I Am Weak

JOHN HOLMES

Foreword by John Gunstone

daybreak

London

First published in 1992 by
Daybreak
Darton, Longman and Todd Ltd
89 Lillie Road, London SW6 1UD

ISBN 0-232-51974-9

A catalogue record for this book is available
from the British Library

Unless otherwise stated the biblical quotations
are taken from the Revised English Bible © 1989
by permission of Oxford and Cambridge University Presses.
Thanks are also due to Constable Publishers
for permission to quote from *Tomorrow is Too Late*
by Ray Moore and to Gill and Macmillan, Dublin,
for extracts from 'Temptation' and 'I like youngsters'
from *Prayers of Life* by Michel Quoist.

Phototypeset by Intype, London
Printed and bound in Great Britain at
the University Press, Cambridge

Contents

Acknowledgements

So many people have contributed to this book. Some appear in its pages but many more do not. Twenty-five years of parish ministry have reaped for me countless lessons of Christian life and living, born in the experience of others, most of whom would consider themselves very ordinary members of the Christian community.

I owe a particular debt to my colleagues in ministry – those I have worked with as curate, vicar and rural dean. This book has grown out of reflection which many of them have shared in and contributed to.

For the writing of the book I am especially grateful to my friends, Roger and Di Wild for the use of their cottage, to Joyce Ryder for her tireless work at the typewriter, to Margaret Cross and Colin Holiday for their help, and to Margaret Bardsley and Peter Loveday for reading the transcript and making useful comments.

Especially I am indebted to my wife Rosemary whose remarks gave rise to the idea for the book and who has shared fully in the joys and struggles that lie at the heart of it.

Foreword

John Holmes is an Anglican priest who for the last twenty-five years has ministered in and around the city of Leeds. Nurtured in the Anglo-Catholic tradition, he tried to apply the lessons of that great movement in the parishes to which he was appointed. But he found – as many of us like him have found – that something seemed to be missing from that tradition as our generation has received it.

Then with his wife, Rosemary, he encountered the charismatic renewal, and a new love and power began to manifest itself through his ministry. The Holy Spirit brought a new vitality to his faith and practice – and also led him to a wider and more glorious vision of Jesus Christ as Lord of the Church. He shared that vision with his inner city congregation in Holbeck, and with those in his present parish in Cross Gates, with remarkable results.

Yet he also experienced what it means to go with the Lord on the road to Calvary. He tells us of the sorrows as well as the joys of being called by God to serve his people – sorrows caused by personal tragedies in his own life as well as by those in the lives of the people he pastored.

It is this perspective which sets his book apart from many others of its kind. *When I Am Weak* is not written by a miracle-hungry charismatic looking for signs and wonders. Rather, it is refreshingly honest, showing John's struggles to follow the Holy Spirit in the daily routine of a parish priest and the blessings which stem from them.

This led him to reflect more deeply on those passages from the Old and New Testament which find their focus on two of

Christ's injunctions to his disciples: 'Take up (your) cross daily
and follow me', and 'Receive the Holy Spirit'. Through these
reflections, he came to realise how Scripture and experience
are woven together, so that the Word of God comes alive and
relevant amidst all the changing scenes of life.

And so we learn with him that, to enter into Christ's victory,
we must come to the point where we accept completely that in
everything we are utterly dependent on the Lord. Only then
can we be strong in Spirit. Hence the title of his book.

It is a lesson for us all. There cannot be many readers who,
if they are as honest with themselves as John has been, will
not be enlightened and encouraged by this book.

JOHN GUNSTONE

Introduction

Graham Marshall has failed. The promotion he thought was his has gone to someone else. The company has overlooked him for a younger man. Now he must tell Lesley his wife. What will she think? What will she say? She is stunned. But when she gathers herself, she looks at him and says, 'I forgive you for failing, Graham!'

Graham and Lesley Marshall are fictional characters in the Michael Caine film *Shock to the System*. But the reality is plain enough. Failure is a shock to the system. It is a sign of weakness and weakness is out. The very word has negative associations. The weak-kneed lack resolution. The weak-minded are stupid. The weak point is when we are most prone to succumb. 'Surely the weak shall perish, and only the fit survive!'

And so it seems. The weak go to the wall economically, politically, personally. Western nations celebrate the superior strength of their capitalist economic system, while former Communist regimes in Eastern Europe bemoan the weakness and inefficiency of state-run socialism. Political leaders emphasise enterprise and opportunity, so that those with 'talent, hard work and good fortune' (to quote John Major) can thrive. Left-wing voices make much the same sound. 'Fraternity gets eclipsed as Labour grasps opportunity', *The Guardian* headlines a report about the British Labour Party's 1991 policy review 'Opportunity Britain'. Freedom and justice are still proclaimed but the Socialist party seeks to respond positively to the enterprise culture of Western society. The strong and the successful are honoured.

It seems, as Archbishop Desmond Tutu has observed, that

the worst thing that can happen to anyone these days is to fail. We admire those who succeed. It does not matter in what they succeed. Those who are considered failures are looked down upon and most of us will do anything so long as we are not stigmatised as failures. We work hard engaging in the rat-race until stomach ulcers have become status symbols. You are acceptable as long as you succeed.[1]

Such attitudes so prevalent in society can also be found in the life of the church. Christians suffering from depression can be seen as failures, as if faith inevitably dispels weakness of any kind. There is much talk of victory in some Christian circles – but little understanding of failure. We hear of the Spirit who fills his people with love and joy and peace, but hear less of the Spirit who sometimes leads his people as he led Jesus into the wilderness, where they can *face* weakness, pain, failure rather than run away from them. Bishop David Young, until recently the president of the worldwide Christian society SPCK, when speaking to the clergy of his own diocese emphasised the cost of such unbalanced teaching:

We have laid tremendous stress upon the teaching of the resurrection and the experience of the living, risen Lord . . . Now that's fine provided that in restoring resurrection we do not lose crucifixion. I hear in parts of the world . . . a teaching which says that Jesus will not let you suffer. All problems will be solved, they will vanish. I do not believe that to be true and I do not believe that that is the Jesus who calls us to take up our cross and follow Him. There has to be in our teaching this notion that the way of Jesus, the way of discipleship is inevitably the way of the cross. That is the recognition of the hurt and pain at the heart of existence and at the heart of our own personal lives. I've come across clergy and families in this diocese that I believe have been led astray by that doctrine that Jesus will not let me suffer. We do suffer and to belong to him is not to be excused that dimension of human living.

Weakness is part of our experience as Christians. Not just the weakness of sin, but also the weakness of suffering, of failure, of fear and depression, even despair. Yet such weakness will not overwhelm us if we are able to face it – with the grace of Christ. Here surely is the great Christian paradox St Paul expressed when he said, 'When I am weak, then I am strong'.

I shall prefer to find my joy and pride in the very things that are my weakness; and then the power of Christ will come and rest upon me. Hence I am well content, for Christ's sake, with weakness, contempt, persecution, hardship and frustration; for when I am weak, then I am strong.
(2 Cor. 12:9–10 NEB)

To acknowledge our weakness is so often the breakthrough. To acknowledge weakness to ourselves – and to God can lead to a fresh awareness of his grace. Robert Warren speaks for many when he says, 'My conviction which has arisen both from the study of scripture and from reflection on my own experience, is that for the Christian *learning takes place at the point of weakness!*'[2]

And so does Christian growth. Gerard Hughes in *God of Surprises* comments:

If God is my rock, my refuge and my strength then I have no need to be defensive, for I know he accepts me as I am and I am precious in his eyes, that his power is greatest in my weakness and that it is through my weakness that I come to a knowledge of my true identity and worth, called before the world was, to be at one with him in whom all things exist.[3]

Finding new strength in our weakness has implications not just for our personal lives, but also for the life of the church and for society. All is not as it seems. The achievement-success ethic of our times is getting a worn look, even for our economics. As a journalist has written, 'Real capitalism is not just West Germany and Sweden and Japan and the boutiques along Madison Avenue, it is also Brazil and Mexico and the Philippines and the homeless along Madison Avenue'.

It is into that world, broken and breaking that the church is called to be the body of Christ. But even that calling is a reminder of our weakness. 'My friends, think what sort of people you are, whom God has called. Few of you are wise by any human standard, few powerful or of noble birth. Yet, to shame the wise, God has chosen what the world counts folly, and to shame what is strong, God has chosen what the world counts weakness' (1 Cor. 1:26,27).

St Paul was writing to the church in Corinth, but his words are an eternal reminder that God stands with the weak. As we acknowledge our weakness to him and to each other, so he can and does use us by his grace for the renewal of his creation. 'He has chosen things without rank or standing in the world, mere nothings, to overthrow the existing order' (1 Cor. 1:28).

Feeling weak? Seeking to help those who are? Then read on. Let us discover together how we can grow strong precisely in and through those places of weakness.

1

Nothing to offer

'When the pressure is on, the weaknesses begin to appear!'
The commentator was describing a critical moment in a tennis
match. He could have been describing my own situation as a
parish priest that Tuesday morning.

I was on my way to Mirfield, the home of the Community
of the Resurrection. Two days later I was due to speak at a
renewal meeting next door to the Community at the Church
of Christ the King, Battyeford. The meeting was one of a
regular series organised by some of the Mirfield Fathers. I was
supposed to be taking some people from my parish with me.
Our theme: parish renewal. Our story: an inner city parish in
Leeds, experiencing new life and new growth. But now I knew
I could not go. The leadership of the church was in turmoil.
So was I.

'I have nothing to offer you but my weakness', I said to the
three Mirfield Fathers, once I had arrived. There was a pause.
'Well offer us that then!' For a moment I looked in blank
astonishment. But then one of them explained. When they had
prayed together earlier that morning, one of them had seen in
their mind's eye a priest's wafer for the Eucharist being offered
to God. But this large round Communion wafer was not whole.
It was broken in two. Yet still the priest's hands held it in
offering. 'It seems as if God is saying', the monk explained,
'offer your brokenness to me – and I will use it.'

I had never received such an extraordinary invitation before
– or so it seemed. Now my brief for the meeting was not to
talk about parish renewal, but to offer my weakness. Somehow

sensing that God was in all this, with great reluctance I agreed to return two days later. But what would I say?

The weakness I felt then was not primarily the weakness of sin – I knew that often enough. It was rather a feeling of failure, disappointment, hurt – all rolled into one. I had been let down – and I had let down myself. Five years of ministry in my present parish seemed in the balance. Three and a half years especially when so many good things had happened in so many ways seemed in danger of being lost. This was no ordinary problem of parish ministry. I had twelve years' experience of that. This was a serious crisis.

There was a breakdown of relationships among key church leaders. My own leadership was under attack. Two of the worship leaders had told me they had lost confidence in me and would not work with me. Fundamental disagreements had emerged after a time of great strain. It was a situation that was to reach a painful resolution sometime later. But then I felt the full weight of it in my whole being. I felt broken. I was weak.

But that was hardly edifying material for a gathering of Christian people eager to hear something helpful and encouraging. If I was to speak of weakness, surely I had to share some Christian insight or understanding which could offer help to others.

So I turned to the Bible – or to be more precise to my Bible concordance – and looked up the references for weak and weakness. I was surprised to discover there were so many. As I began to look them up in my Bible, I found verses familiar to me suddenly took on a new relevance.

'Be merciful to me, O Lord, for I am weak' (Ps. 6:2 NEB) summed up my prayer well. The psalmist may have been praying from sickness. But it is just as likely his weakness was a result of adversity or opposition. 'A Prayer for Help in Time of Trouble' is the Good News Bible's summary of the psalm's content and its racy translation fitted well my mood.

Give me strength; I am completely exhausted
and my whole being is deeply troubled. (Ps. 6:2, 3 GNB)

But then often in Scripture God is the one who does give
strength.

He gives vigour to the weary,
new strength to the exhausted.
Young men may grow weary and faint,
even the fittest may stumble and fall;
but those who look to the Lord will win new strength,
they will soar as on eagles' wings;
they will run and not feel faint,
march on and not grow weary.

(Isa. 40:29–31)

In the film *Chariots of Fire* those verses were read by the
actor Ian Charlesworth portraying the Scottish athlete and
Christian Eric Liddell against scenes of young Olympic athletes
competing, sometimes falling and invariably ending exhausted.
'Those who look to the Lord will win new strength'.

Yet even in Jesus we see one who did look to the Lord and
yet felt weak. In Gethsemane we hear his words, 'The spirit is
willing, but the flesh is weak' (Matt. 26:41). St Luke's account
goes on to describe how an angel came to strengthen him while
in his anguish of spirit he prayed more and more fervently and
his sweat fell to the ground like drops of blood (Luke 22:43–4).
In his weakness which Jesus openly expressed to his Father, he
found strength to embrace his Father's will.

In Scripture it is St Paul though who most often speaks of
weakness. He had a special concern for the weak. 'We would
urge you brothers, to admonish the careless, encourage the
faint-hearted, support the weak, and to be very patient with
them all' (1 Thess. 5:14 NEB). He explains how for the sake
of the gospel, 'To the weak I became weak, to win the weak'
(1 Cor. 9:22).

Paul did not just speak of others' weakness, he referred to

his own. Sometimes it is the weakness he shares with us all. Like weakness in prayer. 'We do not even know how we ought to pray', yet he affirms, '. . . the Spirit comes to the aid of our weakness' (Rom. 8:26). This was not just correct doctrine but a living experience for Paul. Writing to the church at Corinth he describes how anxious, weak and fearful he felt on his first visit to them, but 'I resolved that while I was with you I would think of nothing but Jesus Christ – Christ nailed to the cross. I came before you weak, nervous and shaking with fear' (1 Cor. 2:2, 3 NEB). The great apostle to the Gentiles shares his own weakness, not to indulge himself or his hearers but to point to the true source of strength.

Paul was to make the same point in an even more dramatic way when he wrote in 2 Corinthians of the serious difficulties he and his companions encountered in Asia. Paul had felt weak and helpless in the face of this crushing experience, 'Indeed, we felt in our hearts that we had received a death sentence' (2 Cor. 1:9). Whether his hearers would have known to what he referred we cannot tell. Various suggestions have been made, but Paul's argument is more fundamental. 'This was meant to teach us to place reliance not on ourselves, but on God who raises the dead. From such mortal peril God delivered us; and he will deliver us again, he on whom our hope is fixed' (2 Cor. 1:9, 10). As we admit our weakness to God and place our reliance on him, so we can discover again his deliverance.

For the most part Paul is hesitant to refer to his own experience, preferring rather to set forward the crucified and risen Lord and all the implications of our life in him. But at times challenged by criticism, he takes us more deeply into himself. He reveals the extent of his hurt. He leads us to the springs of his faith. He shares his experience of God in his weakness.

To the church at Corinth he feels he has to defend his apostleship against those he describes as 'sham apostles, confidence tricksters masquerading as apostles of Christ' (2 Cor. 11:13). He is hurt, but he will speak out even though he is foolish to do so. 'I am mad to speak like this, but I can outdo them'

(2 Cor. 11:23). There follows a most extraordinary catalogue of suffering for the gospel:

> more often overworked, more often imprisoned, scourged more severely, many a time face to face with death. Five times the Jews have given me the thirty-nine strokes; three times I have been beaten with rods; once I was stoned; three times I have been shipwrecked, and for twenty-four hours I was adrift on the open sea. I have been constantly on the road; I have met dangers from rivers, dangers from robbers, dangers from my fellow countrymen, dangers from foreigners, dangers in the town, dangers in the wilderness, dangers at sea, dangers from false Christians. I have toiled and drudged and often gone without sleep; I have been hungry and thirsty and have often gone without food; I have suffered from cold and exposure.
>
> Apart from these external things, there is the responsibility that weighs on me every day, my anxious concern for all the churches. (2 Cor. 11:23–8)

Paul has been forced against his better instincts to boast. But he is clear what he will boast about. 'Is anyone weak? I share his weakness . . . If boasting there must be, I will boast of the things that show up my weakness' (2 Cor. 11:29a, 30). Then he takes us further into himself. 'I come now to visions and revelations granted by the Lord' (2 Cor. 12:1). Speaking in the third person of a Christian man, but obviously referring to himself, Paul describes the vision he had, when he was caught up to the third heaven which according to late Jewish belief was the highest heaven of all. Yet he recounts this experience with reluctance and real reticence – and the reason he speaks at all is only to reinforce his basic point.

> To keep me from being unduly elated by the magnificence of such revelations, I was given a thorn in my flesh, a messenger of Satan sent to buffet me; this was to save me from being unduly elated. Three times I begged the Lord to rid

me of it, but his answer was: 'My grace is all you need, power is most fully seen in weakness.' (2 Cor. 12:7–9a)

Christian theologians through the centuries and Bible scholars today debate what the 'thorn in the flesh' refers to. At one time it was taken to mean something outside of himself – like opposition or persecution – but most would maintain today that the trouble was essentially physical. Epilepsy, malaria, stammering and blindness have all been suggested. Certainly the 'thorn in the flesh' was debilitating, frustrating and a cause of great difficulty to Paul. Yet here Paul boasts of it, for as God had shown him, 'my power is made perfect in weakness' (2 Cor. 12:9 RSV).

Paul is able to conclude,

I shall therefore prefer to find my joy and pride in the very things that are my weakness; and then the power of Christ will come and rest upon me. Hence I am well content, for Christ's sake, with weakness, contempt, persecution, hardship, and frustration; for when I am weak, then I am strong. (2 Cor. 12:9b–10 NEB)

So Paul unveils the great Christian paradox of strength in weakness, a paradox rooted in his own experience of God, 'When I am weak, then I am strong'.

When I read those words in my own weakness, their truth seemed to penetrate me in a deeper way than ever before. As if a key had been turned and a door opened to a deeper understanding of the way of God in our weakness, I was being invited not to deny my weakness or run away from it but face it. Then admitting it to myself, I would be able to admit it to God. Fresh light was thrown not just on my present situation, but also on earlier events and difficulties. Maybe if I could fully acknowledge my weakness, God would teach me new lessons of his grace and power, lessons which would take me forward – yes and the church too – in his service.

The renewal meeting beckoned. I set off armed with my

Bible, my notes on Paul and three people from the parish who at very short notice I had asked to speak of how they had known God's strength in their weakness. I did not speak of my own experience. Rather I spoke of St Paul – and how he had known God's power in his weakness. I took the well-attended meeting through the various passages of Scripture – and showed how for St Paul, 'When I am weak, then I am strong'. I asked my three friends from St Luke's Holbeck, where I was vicar at the time, to illustrate this same truth from their own experience.

As I spoke I felt as weak as ever. There was no sense of being uplifted, as I shared God's word. But when the meeting had finished, someone who knew me well said, 'I've never heard you speak with such authority'. In my weakness the power of Christ had come and rested upon me. Somehow there was less of John Holmes, and more of Jesus Christ.

I had learnt what St Paul knew. Ministering from my weakness I had found the Lord's strength. Here was a discovery about Christian life and ministry that would have rich implications. Sister Briege McKenna shares the same lesson in her book *Miracles Do Happen*.

She tells how in February 1980 as her mind was turning towards a forthcoming visit to Brazil, her father died. He had been a great support to her throughout her life and ministry. Though she now lived with other sisters of the international Order of St Clare in the USA and her father was still in her native Ireland, his death had a profound effect on Sister Briege.

It was a very sad moment for all of us. Because of the change in schedule and the need to be with my family, I was unable to prepare adequately for a month of ministry to priests and laity. On my way to Brazil, since I felt I was so unprepared I asked Jesus to accept my emptiness and the suffering caused by my father's death.

In spite of my lack of preparation I felt this was one of my most powerful missions, because I had nothing of my own. Out of my poverty, I had to let the Lord work.[1]

It is an 'amazing and true fact of life', as Dr William Barclay observed, 'that it is the people who realize their own weakness, their own lack of wisdom, their own helplessness and powerlessness, who in the end are strong and wise'. Time and again Christian people have discovered that it is at the point of acknowledged weakness that strength comes and new understanding.

'I have nothing to offer except my weakness!' Maybe that is the sum total of what you feel you can offer at the moment. Recovering from tragedy, handling great difficulty, facing a critical time and feeling so inadequate or just weighed down by suffering or sin, you know well your weakness. Then see that not as disqualification for Christian service or a reason to flee from the challenge of Christian living. See it rather as an opportunity for breakthrough to a deeper awareness of God and his resources and a greater effectiveness precisely in those parts of your life where you feel least capable. Offer your weakness to God. Go with your empty hands and present yourself to him. In a moment of quiet self-surrender open your heart, yourself to his love and grace. Learn what Carlo Carretto has discovered. 'God can do everything and I can do nothing. But if I offer this nothing in prayer to God, everything becomes possible in me'.[2]

2

The wounded healer

'Is there anyone you specially want me to look out for?' the hospital chaplain was asking the ward sister, before he began his weekly visiting round. 'Yes there is', she answered. 'The woman in the end bed. She's very bitter, especially against God. I doubt whether she will allow you to speak to her.'

The chaplain followed his usual practice of speaking to all the patients on the ward, apart from those asleep or being tended to. People were pleased to share a few moments with him or have a longer chat when it seemed necessary. As he approached the end bed, though, the woman turned away from him. 'Don't come near me! Don't talk to me!' she barked. 'God's got me in a trap!' The chaplain attempted to respond, but the woman was adamant. 'God's got me in a trap!'

The following week on his way to the hospital, the chaplain called in at a little shop nearby that sold Christian books, prayer cards, ornaments and the like. He bought a small crucifix, just the right size to hold in your hand, and took it with him to the ward. The woman was still there in the end bed. Physically she was a little weaker than before, but she still called out to the chaplain as he approached. 'Don't come near me! God's got me in a trap!' This time he did not try to argue. He just moved forward quickly, put the crucifix into the woman's hand and said, 'God's in the trap with you.' Then he left.

When he visited the ward next week, the sister was looking out for him. 'Something remarkable has happened in the ward this week', she told him eagerly. 'The woman in the end bed. She died three days ago. She had been very poorly. But what was remarkable was this. She died not bitter, but serene. Somehow all the bitterness seemed to drain away from her. And she never let go of that crucifix.'

A picture, they say, is worth a thousand words. Was it that image of the crucified Christ that pierced through the hard shell of bitterness, revealing to that dying woman the presence of God with her? Did she realise in some deeper than merely intellectual way that because Jesus 'himself has passed through the test of suffering, he is able to help those who are in the midst of their test'? (Heb. 2:18) Certainly something happened and a profound change took place.

But when we recognise Jesus as the wounded healer we won't be surprised. The one who suffered and died on the cross is able to enter into and share the suffering of his people. Jesus is not 'incapable of feeling our weaknesses with us' (Heb. 4:15 JB). Rather he 'has been tested in every way as we are, only without sinning' (Heb. 4:15).

The Wounded Healer is the title of a study of ministry in contemporary society by Fr Henri Nouwen. The book grew out of lectures originally given at Yale Divinity School. Fr Nouwen sought to explain the true nature of a Christian minister as a wounded healer. He said:

After so much stress on the necessity of a leader to prevent his own personal feelings and attitudes interfering in a help-ing relationship, it seems necessary to re-establish the basic principle that no-one can help anyone without becoming involved, without entering with his whole person into the painful situation, without taking the risk of becoming hurt, wounded or even destroyed in the process. The beginning and end of all Christian leadership is to give your life for others. Thinking about martyrdom can be an escape unless we realise that real martyrdom means a witness that starts with the willingness to cry with those who cry, laugh with those who laugh and to make one's own painful and joyful experiences available as sources of clarification and under-standing.[1]

Jesus is the embodiment of that basic principle. He is the wounded healer. He enters with his whole person into the painful situation of humanity. He takes the risk of becoming hurt, wounded, even destroyed. He does give his life for others. He does cry with those who cry, he does laugh with those who laugh – and his painful and joyful experiences are indeed for us sources of clarification and understanding and healing.

And they are so precisely because in Jesus we are encountering the very nature and being of God. 'God is Christlike and in him is no unChristlikeness at all',[2] as Bishop Michael Ramsey has expressed the fundamental truth of the incarnation. The weakness and suffering that Jesus entered into and shared with a weak, suffering humanity is a demonstration that 'God is the fellow-sufferer who understands'. 'No one has ever seen God; God's only Son, he who is nearest to the Father's heart, has made him known' (John 1:18). At the heart of God is the suffering love of the Cross. There God hurts and shares our hurt.

But the open, vulnerable, suffering Jesus is seen not only on the Cross, but throughout his life and ministry. Jesus is not just crucified as our wounded healer. He is born that way. He reveals that nature in his life and ministry in Galilee, as well as in his suffering and death in Jerusalem. From day one we encounter Jesus the wounded healer, sharing our painful situation, open and vulnerable to the world.

The Basilica of the Nativity in Bethlehem stands over the traditional site of the birthplace of Jesus. As you approach the church from Manger Square it has a rather forbidding appearance, looking more like a fortress than a place of worship. But then to enter, you have to stoop. The entrance is only 3'6" high. It was made that way to prevent people riding into church on horseback. But it is a reminder today of the need for us to bow low in worship before the incarnate Lord. It reminds us too of God's lowliness and humility in becoming incarnate, born in the flesh for us and all people. There is in the birth of Jesus a special vulnerability.

St Luke's Gospel shows us that. Jesus is born in a stable

because there was no room in the inn. He is laid in a manger for a cot. He is visited by shepherds whose very occupation makes them unable to keep the details of ceremonial law and so stand outside orthodox Jewry. From the beginning of his earthly life Jesus is identified with the weak and defenceless. The Christian writer Monica Furlong has said,

> I believe that the kernel of the joy and happiness of Christmas lies in the vulnerability of Jesus. He arrived in the world as naked and helpless as all the rest of us, but unlike the rest of us, remained for the whole of his life without defences. For we, as a result of painful experiences in childhood or later, fence ourselves round with various devices to keep other human beings at bay. We feel that love is a risky business in which we may get hurt, so that we must love with elaborate caution and be careful not to squander affection on those outside our own class, our own race, our own colour, our own moral background, our own family. Gradually we love less and become more and more lonely until as a substitute for love, we need to console ourselves with work, or possessions, or success, or status or lust. One of the glories of Christmas is that it reminds us that nothing really works for us except opening our lives and our hearts to other people . . . It seems that the love and openness of Jesus showed us some fundamental truth about ourselves and the way to live joyfully and that when we deny this truth, then we move towards neurosis and despair.

The angel describes the birth of Jesus as 'good news, news of great joy for the whole nation' (Luke 2:10). It is good news that in the fact and circumstances of the birth of Jesus there is the very presence of almighty God come to stand with us and strengthen us in our weakness and lead us to the springs of joy. His openness is the key to our own.

The same open vulnerable Jesus we see in the babe of Bethlehem we encounter too in the man of Galilee. He is open to the needs of the crowd. He is vulnerable to their demands.

In Matthew 9:36 we read how 'the sight of the crowds moved him to pity; they were like sheep without a shepherd, harassed and helpless'. In the original this means the pain went through his heart. As Jürgen Moltmann has said, 'He could not get the existence and situation of the people out of his mind, nor could he restrain the people from pressing around him. Their suffering came to him, went into him, so that he had to – and wanted to – identify with them'.[3]

And so he does in what has been described as the 'inexhaustible activity of Galilee, redemptive and life giving'.[4] His word, his touch, his love bring life, wholeness and freedom to those who seek him. There is a contagious life-giving power that people find in Jesus, in his openness and availability to them. To the blind beggar Bartimaeus Jesus asks, 'What do you want me to do for you?' He makes himself wholly available to one whose blindness has caused his poverty (Mark 10:51). To the superintendent of taxes Zacchaeus Jesus says, 'I must stay at your house today'. To one alone and friendless whose occupation as a tax-collector made him both corrupt and treacherous in people's eyes, Jesus offers his transforming friendship (Luke 19:5). To the woman with the haemorrhages who touches him, Jesus says, 'Daughter, your faith has healed you. Go in peace!' He offers his healing love to someone whose condition took her outside conventional religion and who had fallen trembling at his feet. His tender compassion is put at the service of all who come to him in need. But in such a generous ministry there is a deep cost: 'everyone in the crowd was trying to touch him, because power went out from him and cured them all' (Luke 6:19).

Jesus was only able to sustain such openness to the needs of others, because of his relationship to his Father. Time with the crowds is balanced by time alone in prayer. An evening of responsiveness to the needs of others is followed by an early morning of quiet withdrawal.

That evening after sunset they brought to him all who were ill or possessed by demons; and the whole town was there, gathered at the door. He healed many who suffered from various diseases, and drove out many demons . . . Very early next morning he got up and went out. He went away to a remote spot and remained there in prayer. (Mark 1:32–5)

Jesus needs to be alone with his Father, receiving fresh inspiration and guidance for his ministry. It sets a limit on his availability to particular people (see Luke 4:42–3).

We get a richer picture of the vulnerability of Jesus when we realise that he is not inexhaustible. He does get tired, as we do. He does need to be alone and receive fresh strength in quiet, as we do. He has to battle with temptation, as we do. It is the Spirit who leads Jesus out into the wilderness, for there Jesus knows and shares in our weakness. There he is strengthened to be a source of help and healing to others (Matt. 4:1, Mark 1:2, Luke 4:1).

As he offers himself open and vulnerable to others, so he cries with those who cry and rejoices with those who rejoice. As our wounded healer, he makes 'his own painful and joyful experiences available as sources of clarification and healing'.

When the seventy-two return jubilant from their time in the towns and villages he was to visit himself, we see Jesus' own jubilation. 'I thank you, Father, Lord of heaven and earth, for hiding these things from the learned and wise, and revealing them to the simple' (Luke 10:21). Jesus speaks of the joy in heaven over one sinner who repents and demonstrates that joy as he gains a reputation for 'welcoming sinners and eating with them' (see Luke 15:1–7). He refers to such criticisms himself when he says, 'The Son of Man came, eating and drinking, and you say "Look at him! A glutton and a drinker, a friend of tax-collectors and sinners!" ' (Luke 7:34) But then the joyful picture of the heavenly banquet was one of his favourite images for the kingdom of God. The one who came to bring life to all in its fullness knew the joy of life itself and its simple pleasures.

But he knew too the pain of life – and its cost. The Letter to the Hebrews describes how 'in the course of his earthly life he offered up prayers and petitions, with loud cries and tears,

to God who was able to deliver him from death' (Heb. 5:7).
This refers primarily to Jesus' agony in Gethsemane. But Jesus
wept at other times too.

He wept for Jerusalem. When he came in sight of the city
his heart broke over it. 'If only you had known this day the
way that leads to peace!' (Luke 19:42)

He wept when visiting Mary and Martha after the death of
Lazarus. St John vividly portrays the depth of Jesus' emotion:

When Jesus saw her [Mary] weeping and the Jews who had
come with her weeping, he was moved with indignation and
deeply distressed. 'Where have you laid him?' he asked.
They replied 'Come and see'. Jesus wept. The Jews said,
'How dearly he must have loved him!' But some of them
said, 'Could not this man, who opened the blind man's eyes,
have done something to keep Lazarus from dying?' Jesus,
again deeply moved, went to the tomb. (John 11:33–8)

The word used for Jesus' weeping is different from that used
to describe the formal weeping of the Jews. Jesus 'sheds tears'
and shares genuine human emotions of grief and sorrow. Many
of us will have wept with those who weep after the loss of
someone much loved, as Jesus did. But in his tears we see a
God whose heart is wrung with anguish at the anguish of his
people.

Jesus' deep distress is mingled with real indignation. Different translations have struggled to convey the true sense of verse
33 where Jesus is 'deeply moved in spirit and troubled' (RSV)
'with a sigh that came straight from the heart' (JB). Jesus sighs
at the slowness of the Jews to believe despite all they had seen.
William Temple in his *Readings in St John's Gospel* believes
also that Jesus' deep emotion was partly because 'He is preparing for a mighty act of power. His "signs" were not wrought
without cost to Him. There was self-giving in them; and when
a sufferer drew healing from him without His knowledge, He
was conscious "that the power proceeding from him had gone
forth" (Mark 5:30).'[5]

Certainly his agony in Gethsemane cost him dear. The prophet Isaiah describes the servant as 'a man of sorrows, and acquainted with grief' (Isa. 53:3 RSV). That was Jesus' experience, as he took Peter, James and John with him. 'Distress and anguish overwhelmed him'. He turns for their support. 'My heart is ready to break with grief. Stop here and stay awake with me.' He throws himself down on the ground and prays. He is acutely aware of his weakness. 'The spirit is willing, but the flesh is weak' (Matt. 26:37–41).

What causes his agony is not just the prospect of suffering, but also the challenging reality of evil. Some have said his physical agony on the Cross was not so crushing as his agony of spirit in the Garden. Certainly he tasted to the full in Gethsemane the depths to which human envy and prejudice and bigotry could bring humanity down. He bore the whole tragedy of the human situation in his own spirit, as later he was to bear it on the Cross.

1990 saw the first production of a new play by Peter Barnes called *Sunsets and Glories* set against the backcloth of thirteenth century Italy. The central character is Peter de Morrone, the saintly Pope Celestine V. He contrasts the church and her Lord.

> Christ was poor, we are rich. Christ was meek and low, we are tall and proud. Christ forsook earthly glory, we hold it fast. Christ washed his disciples' feet, we make men kiss ours. Christ came to serve, we seek to be served. Christ purchased heaven, we give the earth to the rich. Christ rode on an ass, we on fat palfreys. Christ gave power, we grapple it close. Christ loosened, we bind. Christ brought life, we bring death.[6]

The death of Christ is life-giving. Jesus, the wounded healer, wounded by our sins, makes the offering of his life our source of healing. 'He carried our sins in his own person on the gibbet, so that we might cease to live for sin and begin to live for righteousness. By his wounds, you have been healed' (1 Pet.

2:24). That life always lived open and vulnerable to others, always responsive to the Father's will, reaches its appropriate climax on Golgotha. 'When I am lifted up from the earth, I shall draw everyone to myself' (John 12:32).

Like wandering sheep, we have been sought out and brought back to him. And coming to him with all our wounds and weakness we can trust ourselves to his care. 'Unload all your worries on to him, since he is looking after you' (1 Pet. 5:7 JB). His love beckons from his open heart.

One of the leaders in a church I served was a widow called Margaret. A life-long believer, her own Christian faith had been gently renewed one Holy Week. Several years later she became responsible for overseeing the ministry of healing in the church and she was much used by God both as a pastor and in her prayers. But then a health problem she had had for a while began to get worse. It was an illness that affected her balance and her vision. Things began to go seriously awry after a spell in hospital. For a time she was completely confined to her home, unable even to read or watch television, sitting for the most part in a darkened room. She seemed trapped. I called to see her one particularly busy day for me – and there she was in her chair sitting erect and still (on doctor's orders) with nothing whatever to occupy her or distract her. She said to me, 'I've only Jesus to rely on.' Her awareness of Jesus with her in her enforced stillness contrasted with my own lack of peace in my busyness. Though later she was to make a full physical recovery, it was her openness to Jesus with her in her suffering that revealed to me again how his power 'is made perfect in weakness'.

Angela faced a different problem. It only came to light well on in her adult life, even though its origins were in her child-hood. Angela was brought up to fear God. Not the fear the Bible commends to us, that recognition of who God is, perfect in power, love and purity and reverence before him. Such a 'fear of the Lord is the beginning of wisdom and they who live by it grow in understanding' (Ps. 111:10). Angela's fear was an unwholesome dread. God was perceived as a stern headmaster,

unrelenting, exacting and distant, and a dread of him took deep
hold on her personality. As she grew into adulthood, she drifted
away from the church of her childhood. Later she came to a
new deeper Christian commitment in a different church from
the one she had been brought up in. In this church God was
known to smile at times. Yet still her fear wreaked its own
private havoc in her life, filling her with periodic anxiety and
frequent visits to the doctor and various medications. Then one
weekend at her church a visiting team from another parish was
the means of her breakthrough. Through counsel and prayer
the root cause of her anxiety was identified and an inward
release took place. Jesus the wounded healer brought his own
healing to her spirit and enabled her to see in the face of God
not a figure of terror but a loving Lord who reached out to her
in warm embrace. Angela began a new chapter in her life. She
knew a new security within her and the weeks, months and
years since have borne out the change he effected.

One of the words most often on the lips of Jesus is 'Come!'
'Come to me, all who are weary and whose load is heavy; I
will give you rest' (Matt. 11:28). 'Come, follow me,' he says
to the first disciples (Mark 1:17). 'Come,' he says to Peter in
the boat (Matt. 14:29). 'Let the children come to me' (Mark
10:14). 'Come with me', he says to all who will heed his call.
And as in his earthly ministry, so today 'anyone who comes to
me I will never turn away' (John 6:37). His invitation is there
for all. Whatever trap we feel ourselves in, he can be inside it
with us. Whatever fear paralyses our life, his gentle understanding love can be the source of our liberation. He knows his way
around the wrecks and wounds of our humanity, and in his
care our weakness can be turned to strength. 'Come', says
Jesus, the wounded healer. Paul in his weakness was able to
say, 'I have the strength to face all conditions by the power
that Christ gives me' (Phil. 4:13 GNB). Let us heed Jesus'
invitation and find new strength and healing in him.

3

Facing suffering

The cards and telegrams were being read out at the wedding reception. At the point when attention usually flags, suddenly we sat up. The couple were receiving greetings from a mutual friend, 'May you have the wisdom of Solomon, the patience of Job and the children of Israel.'

The patience of Job is famous. His comforters are infamous. Eliphaz, Bildad and Zophar are described as Job's 'three friends come to condole with him and comfort him'. They produce lengthy arguments to assail Job's professed innocence. Job is not impressed, and nor are we. 'How long will you grieve me and crush me with words?' (Job 19:2)

But they had not begun like that.

When they first saw him from a distance, they did not recognise him; they wept aloud, tore their cloaks, and tossed dust into the air over their heads. For seven days and seven nights they sat beside him on the ground, and none of them spoke a word to him, for they saw that his suffering was very great. (Job 2:12, 13)

Their first response to Job's suffering was not words, but silence. It is when they started speaking, they let Job down.

We are in the same danger. It is easy to be glib and facile when speaking about suffering. Often silence is the best response.

'What shall I say to her?' The voice at the other end of the phone was a member of the congregation whose sister's husband had just died suddenly and unexpectedly. She confessed,

'I just don't know what to say.' 'Don't bother about that', I responded. 'Just go. Be with her.' Her presence was needed more than her words.

So often that is the case. A priest friend of mine told me about a man from his congregation who rang him one day. The man's wife was in hospital due to have a critical operation. Suddenly this loving husband had felt very alone. 'I wondered if you would see me', he had asked. They arranged to meet at the hospital at the time the operation would be taking place. The priest knew the man well. Small talk did not seem appropriate. 'Shall we go for a walk?' my friend had suggested. It was a dull, cloudy day, but dry and they wandered slowly around the extensive gardens and grounds of the hospital. Not a word was spoken. Eventually the man broke the silence as they approached his wife's ward. He turned to his companion and said, 'Thank you for being such a comfort to me.'

The suffering of others has often filled me with a profound silence. I was shielded from suffering for much of my early life – as many people are these days. I came face to face with it on a regular basis only after having become part-time chaplain at a hospital which was the regional radiotherapy centre for the treatment of cancer. I combined the work with being curate in the local parish. I lived just five minutes' walk from the hospital. I was available for emergencies, but also went in on a regular basis. I took Communion early on Sunday morning and visited the wards on Friday afternoon.

I had not been chaplain there long when one day I saw a young woman of twenty-one die of a very rare form of cancer, that developed as a result of childbirth. The baby lived, but the mother died. For several hours I was with her as spurred on by her distraught husband she hung on to life, until in the end she could hang on no more. The illness had taken its full toll in just a few weeks.

I came back from hospital that day in deep thought. Some children were playing soccer in the pub car park at the end of the road where we lived. Their shouts and enthusiasm jarred, as I sought to grapple intellectually with what I had just witnessed.

A few months later I became concerned about my own health. I went to see my local GP. I seemed to be having a physical problem which began to develop every Thursday and came to a climax on Fridays. He gave me a thorough examination and told me I was in good physical shape. 'Are you under any particular stress at the moment?' he asked. 'Any change of work? Any new responsibility?' He explained how an identical condition to mine had appeared in another of his patients who had recently been promoted to a very responsible post that was much more demanding. As we talked, it soon became obvious that my hospital chaplaincy lay behind my present condition – and in particular my regular Friday afternoon visits to the wards. Facing other people's suffering was causing me inward stress with a physical result. Once I realised that, I was able to offer my situation to God and ask for his strength and healing. The condition soon cleared up. Acknowledging my vulnerability to the suffering of others made me stronger and wiser. Being present at the death of that young mother had not enlightened my understanding except by deepening my questions but it had helped me to be more honest with God – and myself.

Such was the challenge Tony Gardiner faced at a much deeper level after the death of his first wife. When I was a vicar in South Leeds, Tony was the neighbouring minister, pastoring a united Baptist-Methodist-U.R.C. congregation. By the time he arrived in the area, he had married a second time and was beginning a family. But earlier he had lived and worked at Castleford. It was there his first wife was knocked down by a car and killed when they had been married just eighteen months.

He wrote later:

The sense of loss is devastating. It has been likened many times to an amputation, the tearing away of part of oneself, leaving you maimed, crippled, stumbling – and empty, drained of life and purpose. And the loss is absolute. There is no appeal against it. C. S. Lewis, struggling to cope with his

wife's death, wrote: 'I look up at the night sky. Is anything
more certain than that in all those vast times and spaces, if
I were allowed to search them, I should nowhere find her
face, her voice, her touch. She died. She is dead. Is the word
so difficult to learn?'[1]

Tony writes of his own experience in an article 'Confronting
the Abyss: the relationship between bereavement and faith'
and confronting the depth of the loss is one of the lessons he
shares. The pain should be faced. That is both more honest
and in the long run more healing.

Attempts to evade our own pain bring, not peace, but deep-
rooted psychological and emotional disturbance. It becomes
a yet more intolerable anguish which we must bury deeper
and deeper still. A friend lost his only daughter in a road
accident sixteen years ago. He has never spoken of that
daughter, never uttered her name, from that day to this.
Seeking to avoid the pain of grief, he has condemned himself
to a lifetime of torment. One senses the rawness of the
wound even after so many years.

'Faced with our own grief', Tony Gardiner concludes, 'evas-
ive action is not possible. We cannot skirt around the abyss
that opens up before us'.[2]
But in facing the abyss what contribution does faith make?
Confronting such personal suffering, how can Christians
respond with integrity? David Watson, grappling with his own
cancer, surveyed the various arguments put forward to deal
with the perennial problem of suffering. Often he had to conclude, 'I don't know'. 'On many thousands of issues we simply
do not and cannot know . . . Although man has great dignity,
being made in the image of God, he must also appreciate his
smallness and his natural inability to grasp more than a tiny
fraction of total reality'.[3] This willingness to admit 'I don't
know' can be more helpful to the sufferer than the facile or
glib response sometimes made in the name of faith.

A father, scout leader and regular churchgoer, faces the death of one of his children, and is able to reconcile the tragedy with his faith. But the tragic loss of a second child is too much. His faith is shattered. No one is able to console him. No one is able to offer him any Christian counsel or comfort that brings any light to his darkness. No one, that is, except the vicar. 'I'll never forget what he said to me', the father says beginning to recover from his grief. 'When I asked him, "Why if God is as you say a loving Father, could this happen?" he answered, "I don't know".' That honest admission was more helpful than all the wise words he had received.

But is there more that faith can say? At the heart of God is the suffering love of the Cross. Jesus is our wounded healer and in his suffering we can begin to face our own and find a way through it. Elie Wiesel, a survivor of Auschwitz, describes what happened in the camp one day.

The SS hanged two Jewish men and a youth in front of the whole camp. The men died quickly but the death throes of the youth lasted for half an hour. 'Where is God? Where is He?' someone asked behind me. As the youth still hung in torment in the noose after a long time, I heard the man call again, 'Where is God now?' and I heard a voice in myself answer 'Where is He? He is here. He is hanging there on the gallows.'[4]

In the midst of that most appalling of all suffering humanity has known this century God is not seen as distant or unconcerned – but there suffering with his people. In the trap with them.

This is the truth the penitent thief stumbles on unawares in Sydney Carter's song 'Friday Morning'.

It was on a Friday morning that they took me from the cell,
And I saw they had a carpenter to crucify as well.
You can blame it on to Pilate. You can blame it on the
    Jews.

You can blame it on the devil, it's God I accuse!
It's God they ought to crucify instead of you and me,
I said to the carpenter a-hanging on the tree.

You can blame it on to Adam, you can blame it on to Eve,
You can blame it on the apple, but that I can't believe.
It was God that made the devil, and the Woman and the
   Man,
And there wouldn't be an apple if it wasn't in the plan.
It's God they ought to crucify instead of you and me,
I said to the carpenter a-hanging on the tree.

Now Barabbas was a killer and they let Barabbas go.
But you are being crucified for nothing here below.
But God is up in heaven and he doesn't do a thing.
With a million angels watching, and they never move a
   wing.
It's God they ought to crucify instead of you and me,
I said to the carpenter a-hanging on the tree.

To hell with Jehovah, to the carpenter I said,
I wish that a carpenter had made the world instead.
Goodbye and good luck to you, our ways will soon divide.
Remember me in heaven, the man you hung beside.
It's God they ought to crucify instead of you and me,
I said to the carpenter a-hanging on the tree.

But it is God a-hanging on the tree. The crucified carpenter
reveals a crucified God who suffers with his people. 'Only a
suffering God can help'.

Bishop John V. Taylor tells of a visit he was asked to make
to a young couple whose two-year-old daughter had been found
dead in her cot.

They were still stunned and haunted by the old question
Why?, and sometimes, Why her? I simply could not offer
them the conventional reassurance about it all being in God's
providence, a mystery now but one day to be seen as part

of a loving plan. I know that many good souls derive lasting comfort from such counsel, and it certainly squares with a good deal in the Bible, and is to be found in many books of devotion and pastoral practice. But to me it has become unconvincing and strained and suggests a picture of God I find impossible to love, arrogant though that sounds. I said to them instead that their child's death was a tragic accident, an unforeseeable failure in the functioning of the little body; that, so far from being willed or planned by God, it was for him a disaster and a frustration of his will for life and fulfilment, just as it was for them, that God shares their pain and loss and was with them in it. I went on to say that God is not a potentate ordering this or that to happen, but that the world is full of chance and accident and God has let it be so because that is the only sort of world in which freedom, development, responsibility and love could come into being, but that God was committed to this kind of world in love and to each person in it, and was with them in this tragedy, giving himself to them in fortitude and healing and faith to help them through. And their child was held in that same caring, suffering love.[5]

John Taylor encouraged the grieving couple to recognise that God was with them in their tragedy, offering that same caring, suffering love he'd revealed on the Cross.

That was the experience of Rosemary and myself when our fourth child Daniel died in his cot aged five months. An apparently perfectly healthy child when put down for his afternoon sleep. Then soon after dead. A victim of the 'infant cot-death syndrome' as his death certificate said. Still as big a puzzle for today's parents as for us then in 1976. The urgent work of research continues.

But utterly bewildered as we were, we could not blame God for Daniel's death. What sort of a God could have caused such a tragedy? We could not believe that the God we saw in Jesus, and whom we had known so richly in our lives of late could have willed the death of our baby son.

Yet we knew that God was with us, giving himself to us 'in fortitude and healing and faith'. We knew that, when we were still reeling from the shock and stunned. We knew God was with us first in the loving support of other people who came. The friends who sat with us. The neighbour, better with his hands than his words, who was too upset to come in but who said at the vicarage gate, 'I know where you sit'. One of his daughters had been knocked down by a bus and died a few years before. And the bishop who somehow conveyed both the compassion of Christ and the belief that Christ could bring good out of our loss.

We knew God was with us when the day after Daniel died, we somehow faced the full tragedy of his death as a family. With Marianne (9), Patrick (7) and Thomas (5), off school for the day, we sat and talked. We faced the pain and wept together. Daniel had been a joyful child, so much loved by us all. For each of us there was a special grief, for all of us there was much to share.

The involvement of the coroner meant the funeral could not take place for a few days. Daniel had died on a Tuesday. We were able to proceed with his funeral the following Tuesday, but prior to that we felt we wanted to hold a special Eucharist at the church to give thanks for Daniel and commend him to God. We arranged it for the evening, so that as many could come as possible. We knew of the distress and shock not just of family and friends, but also of many people from the church congregation and local community. Daniel had been joyfully baptised just before Christmas in 1975, 'a sign of hope' as our friend Fr Daniel Pearce from Mirfield had proclaimed to our parish congregation in his sermon. Now, had hope died with Daniel? 'Where is God?' so many were asking.

I asked Daniel Pearce to celebrate the Eucharist. Another priest friend led the prayers but I knew I had to preach. Before the service I spoke to the large congregation that gathered and told them not to be afraid to weep. I said I believed we could see Jesus in this service – but not if we tried to deny our feelings. Rosemary and I had chosen the children's song 'Jesus is a friend of mine' to begin the service,

> Jesus is a friend of mine
> Praise Him.

but I'm not sure what was louder, the singing or the sobbing. Yet during the Eucharist we were aware of Jesus' presence with us strongly. He ministered to our broken hearts, he renewed our faith and confidence in him, and after Communion he enabled us to sing – and sing we did in an extraordinary way. The wounded healer was present to heal our wounds. As the service finished, one of the older congregation said to her husband, 'God *is* with us, isn't he!'

Of course there was a burden of suffering to bear long after that evening. The sudden loss of a child, whatever the circumstances, causes wounds that take a long time to heal fully. But God had shown us that our suffering and grief are best borne when it is brought to him, and that he gives us, weak as we are, the power to face them and bear them in his suffering love. 'However deep the pit', Corrie Ten Boom once said, 'God's love is deeper still.' We knew that, as we faced the suffering of our own loss.

The broadcaster Ray Moore faced his own suffering in his struggle with cancer. Best known probably for his programmes on BBC Radio 2, he decided to put pen to paper to help others like himself fighting serious illness. Though not a regular churchgoer in his life or upbringing, he found God's presence with him at his time of need. He was helped to do so by a Salvation Army officer, Harry Read.

Fighting the cancer but submitting to God were two strong lessons taught me recently by Harry Read, the Salvation Army man who had been on hand when I needed him most. He was one of the first people I told of the cancer. By now, of course, he had been promoted higher in the Army and was a very busy man but he dropped everything that day to be with me when I needed his reassuring words. With great understanding he listened to my anger, pain and bewilderment and enabled me, almost by his presence alone to bear the intolerable. He also taught me how to pray. He told me to cup my hands, to imagine them holding all my burdens and my sorrows, and to hand them over physically to God for Him to take.[6]

Shortly after Harry Read wrote a special prayer for Ray Moore to use.

> Lord,
> You know my heart, and how I shrink
> From threat of any further pain.
> How this affects me as I think
> And turmoil starts in me again.
>
> Why cancer, Lord? I'm mystified.
> Why should it strike, and why strike me?
> Why take my cells within its stride
> As though by some divine decree?
>
> But calmer thoughts speak of Your love:
> Remind me that You always care;
> That in the hardest times we prove
> That where we are – the Christ is there.
>
> Though suffering is mystery
> Beyond our power to understand,
> You are life's true reality,
> And courage comes from Your sweet hand.[7]

Discovering the reality of God in his suffering, Ray Moore was able to face his struggle against cancer with deeper honesty and new strength.

Ray Moore was first diagnosed as having cancer when he was 45. Dr Colin MacCallum was 39 when he was told not just that he had cancer, but that he had only a few weeks to live.

The condition was inoperable. The news came as a bombshell to a man who in his wife's words 'never stood still a minute'. He had qualified first as a lawyer and later as a doctor. Now he had a medical practice in North Yorkshire where he lived on a farm with his wife and children. Every minute of his day was consumed by his work as a doctor, keeping up with clinical developments, renovating his farm and caring for his family. Still he felt there was something missing in his life, yet he never seemed to have sufficient time to discover what it was. 'His mind', as his wife Marilyn said later, 'was always open to the possibility of God, but faith was something he could not rationalise.' In his training as a lawyer and a doctor there was always a need for absolute proof or explanatory symptoms so that he could intelligently reach a correct conclusion or diagnosis. God was only a possibility and not something he could prove.

Then suddenly he had only weeks to live. But the weeks gave him time he had never allowed himself before, time to think and thus to find what he had been missing all along. He had been told of his condition towards the end of 1979. In his diary on 9 January 1980 he was able to write, 'My faith is a great comfort to me, and I rejoice in the love of God.' His wife said,

Colin was a very private man and it was completely out of character for him to try to influence people by the way he felt. Nevertheless his shyness vanished beneath the conviction and exultation of his relationship with God. All who visited him expected a broken, sad, dispirited man. Instead, they found him contented, giving a warmth and inspiration as he had never done before, either as a doctor or as a friend. It is strange that Colin, his body weak and dying, and depending completely on others – nurses, doctors, family and friends – proved at his weakest more powerful than ever before in his life. That strength came from outside himself. It could only have come from God.[8]

In his physical weakness Colin MacCallum found a new spiritual strength. God was with him in his suffering, and he rejoiced in God's loving presence. The wounded healer was there to heal, though life was slipping away.

The local vicar, Stuart Burns, prayed for Colin, anointing him and giving him the laying-on-of-hands. A week later when Stuart was again present at the home, Colin's consultant gave him final pain-killing drugs. He told them Colin would probably never regain consciousness. Marilyn asked to be alone with her husband, but within a few minutes a nurse came to summon Stuart. They both witnessed what Marilyn later described.

Colin came totally and completely out of unconsciousness to speak clearly, convincingly and rationally. His face was radiant, healthy and shining strangely white, his eyes wide open and filled with indescribable joy. We were stunned yet elated by the power of the moment. He had a vision of God calling him? Of paradise? Of eternity? He struggled to articulate what he could see – his face and his eyes told more than his words – and spoke clearly: 'I'm going now – I think I'm going now. It's marvellous . . . marvellous . . . it's marvellous'.

His joy was so infectious that we could only laugh with him as we were caught up in his experience. At that moment I felt a great sense of urgency, and almost gladly I encouraged him to go, so that nothing could hold him back.[9]

With so much to live for, so many responsibilities and so much that offered him earthly pleasures, Colin had been ready to die. And when death came, Colin had met it convinced above all of God's love and welcome.

Was Colin's death-bed experience in his final moments of life a product of the powerful drugs he had been administered? Or was it a genuine encounter with the face of eternity and the living God? What is sure is that in his suffering and dying Colin MacCallum became convinced of the reality of God present with him. And this reality reflected not just the truth of Christ's crucifixion, but also the victory of Christ's resurrection. If Jesus

crucified shows us God hurting with his people, Jesus risen
shows us God reigning, alive with his people. And it was that
intense aliveness that Colin seemed particularly aware of as he
died.

But in his resurrection appearances Christ reveals himself to
people every bit as weak as Colin. Colin was physically weak.
Those to whom the risen Christ appears are often emotionally
or spiritually weak, in some sort of negative mood. When Jesus
appears to Mary Magdalene near the tomb she is weeping and
distraught, 'They have taken my Lord away and I do not know
where they have laid him' (John 20:11–16). The disciples in
the upper room are afraid 'behind locked doors for fear of
the Jews' when Jesus comes and stands among them (John
20:19–20). The women who find the empty tomb in Mark's
Gospel leave it terrified (Mark 16:8). The two disciples on the
road to Emmaus are downcast and disillusioned, 'we had been
hoping he was to be the liberator of Israel' (Luke 24:21).
Thomas doubts (John 20:25). But Jesus reveals himself to
them. As his first followers experienced pain, loss, fear and
disillusionment the risen Christ comes. And he comes to us in
our weakness still. As Gerard Hughes has said:

> We can only come to know the risen Christ when we have
> experienced some kind of death, some disillusionment with
> ourselves and others, some loss, bereavement, sense of fear,
> hopelessness or meaningless and have not tried to anaesthe-
> tise ourselves against it. The answer is in the pain, which is
> revealing to us our poverty and our need of God. If we can
> acknowledge and be still in our poverty, Christ will show
> himself to us in his glory.[10]

The wounded healer is our crucified and risen Lord. He
meets us in our personal suffering of illness, loss, anguish or
fear. He bids us share our burden with another, a friend or
minister who can listen without judgement, love without senti-
mentality. He bids us share our burden with him. He bore it
on the Cross, and he bears it still. And in his risen power he

can enable us to bear it and know even there – especially there – something of his glory.

When Eric Liddell, the Olympic athlete and missionary, died in internment in China in 1943, his last words were, 'It's complete surrender!' It is as we completely surrender to God that we can know his compassion – and his power.

4

Hurt

'I know Lord that I am a worm and no man'. A missionary began every prayer with these words when he met with his colleague. He did not just acknowledge his weaknesses, he seemed to wallow in them. 'Lord, I am only a worm', he would say. Eventually his colleague could stand it no longer. He jumped up and said loudly, 'I thank you, Lord, that I am not a worm. I am a man made in your image, and proud of it!'

Thomas Merton has said, 'The root of Christian love is not the will to love, but the faith that one is loved. The faith that one is loved by God.' God's love for us is at the heart of all Christian life and endeavour. Our loving service for him and other people grows out of his loving service for us. 'We love because he loved us first' (1 John 4:19).

So our prayer rightly starts with a recognition of what God has done for us in his love. We are 'fearfully and wonderfully' made, as Psalm 139:14 puts it in the Coverdale translation. He has brought us back to him through the life, death and resurrection of his Son. By the gift of his Spirit he fills us with his life and love.

But sometimes our capacity to receive his love gets blocked. We hurt ourselves by our selfishness and sin and that can block the flow of God's love, until we acknowledge it and ask for God's cleansing forgiveness. The hurts we've received from others, especially those wounds from the past, can also damage our openness to receive from God. The biting remark, the absence of affirmation, the coldness and, for some, physical or sexual abuse leave deep scars. Of course the extent of this damage depends on the depth of the wounds. But some remarks made or attitudes struck can affect us for years, even when their origins seem quite slight.

Garrison Keillor, the American writer and broadcaster, tells of just such an incident from his childhood. It happened when he hit his cousin on the head with a pair of stilts. He refers to his cousin as Abel but that was not his real name.

The stilts were mine. Abel had them, and I grabbed them away, and when he grabbed at me I whacked him with the stilts across the side of his skinny head. He had good presence of mind for a ten year old. When he looked around and saw no adult to appeal to, he turned and said to me in a clear small voice, 'You know what's going to happen to you some-day? You're going to go to prison for the rest of your life.'

The quiet way he said it made me believe him instantly, absolutely. I offered him the stilts and he accepted them, but that didn't change anything. It would be prison for me: no trial, no judge or jury; a policeman would simply pick me up and drive me to the state prison and take me to the children's cellblock. The steel doors would clang shut and the big key turn, the officer's footsteps fade away back down the long concrete hall tap tap tap tap tap toward the light, and not far away a maniacal laugh and the squeaking of mice and water dripping in the dank sewers below. Prison. When you're a little kid, your heart is open and tender and a harsh word can go straight in and become part of your life. I've been living under his sentence for almost forty years now, going along from year to year, waiting, knowing that all the good things I've done won't matter one bit when the cops come and take me away. Once, I was helping Grandma and she said, 'I never saw anyone who could grease a cake pan half as good as you can.' Her kind compliment made me feel talented and useful, and I still feel talented, even competent sometimes, but that doesn't change fate. Probably I'll be making a useful contribution to society right up to the day I go to prison, and then I'll make good license plates.[1]

Of course Garrison Keillor is a humourist, in that rich American tradition of Mark Twain and James Thurber. But in his characteristic way, he touches on an issue that affects so many of us. 'A harsh word can go straight in and become part of your life.'

It was a harsh word and more that a twelve-year-old boy suffered, whom Selwyn Hughes counselled in his adult life. The boy received a Christmas present from his father. When he unwrapped it eagerly, it turned out not to be the train set he had expected – but a brick! As he looked at the 'present' he had been given, the boy's father loomed over him and said, 'That's all you're worth. You've hardly done a thing I've asked you over this past year. Perhaps this will teach you how to behave!' What in fact it did teach him was the strategy, 'I will never again trust anyone or get close to them, for they may disappoint me and let me down.'

When he grew up and married, he found that after a few years his marriage got into serious difficulties. Clearly his strategy not to get too close to anyone in case they disappointed him was destroying his marriage. With Dr Hughes' help he faced the cause of his problems, coming to see in the strength and support of God's love the way through. Gradually he let go of the old strategy, opened his being in a new way to receive God's love, and became in Selwyn Hughes' words 'a transformed person. And more – a transformed husband.'

That is God's desire: to heal the hurts, caused by our sin or others', and make us new. Of course there are many ways this takes place. Sometimes our own life of reflection and prayer yields breakthroughs in understanding and the path to healing is made plain. At other times a wise friend helps us open up difficult experiences in our earlier life and face them in the strength of God's love. Sometimes the help comes through a minister, or healing team. At other times a counsellor, psychotherapist or psychiatrist may be the means of this inner healing. Sometimes it will be various elements of help combined, but always it is God's work. At times he uses them together in a remarkable way.

Dr Paul Tournier tells of a patient he was seeing who had considerable wounds from the past. As he listened, he prayed,

> While I pray in silence, she tells of terrible emotional shocks suffered in childhood, which have weighed on her mind all her life. I cannot, of course, recount them here but what I want to point out is that they are the sort of repressed memories which psychoanalytical technique sometimes helps to bring out into the daylight but never as quickly as this. When I thanked Florence for the trust she had shown in me by being so frank, she replied simply that what had made it possible was that she had come with me into the presence of God.[2]

Being aware of God's presence had given Florence the confidence to uncover her wounds so that she might find healing. When Jesus saw the man, crippled for thirty-eight years, at the pool of Bethesda, he asked him, 'Do you want to be healed?' (John 5:6 RSV) The desire to be healed was present in Florence and that, combined with her confidence in God and in the help of Dr Tournier, unlocked the door for her.

Inner healing – the healing of the wounds and scars from the past – is widely known in the life of the church today. Many times over the last fifteen years or so I have seen such healing in others. It always begins as people are willing to face the weaknesses in their lives and the particular wounds and experiences that lie behind them. Then by patient listening and gentle prayer, I've seen Jesus bring his loving presence deep into a person's life. Often a painful memory lies at the root of a particular problem. Then the recognition that Jesus, 'the same yesterday, today, and for ever' (Heb. 13:8), can touch the past as well as the present has brought in shared reflection or imaginative prayer encounter a new sense of security and well-being.

I think of Abigail, a woman in her mid-thirties who had known much disappointment in her life. She had recently experienced a traumatic divorce. But life began to improve, as she found new friendship and the future seemed less fearful. Then she was tripped up again by a haunting sense that she would be let down. As we were praying with her, we were led back into a painful childhood memory, when she was left alone waiting. Her mother didn't come. As we saw the incident again, we recognised that Jesus was with her in her aloneness and his love would not let her down. Abigail was given confidence to trust herself to a deep relationship once more. She married again and found in her personal and working life a new security, as her awareness of Christ's love for her was deepened and renewed.

I remember Belinda, a young mother handling deep wounds from her father's sexual abuse of her as a child. Help was needed over a period of time but a particular breakthrough came one day. We had re-entered in her imagination the kitchen of her childhood home with her and her father alone. Then Jesus had come into the room, bringing her the warmth of his love and offering his forgiveness to her father. Belinda found a new confidence in her relationship with God and a new attitude to her father. Christ's love began to heal deep wounds.

More recently we were with Charles who in his early forties was able to face again some of the worst memories of his childhood, when drunken violence had played a regular part in his home life. Knowing Jesus' compassion for him when he was five and for his father was an important development in his life as a Christian and with his family. Charles was able to express his love for his father in a way he'd never been able to do before. He told him too he forgave him for the violent scenes of his early life. His father made no comment at the time. A quiet inarticulate man he was able later to say how much he loved his son. He was able to admit to real sorrow at that earlier drunkenness. A profound change has taken place in that family and a new warmth has come to fill the coldness.

In the prophecy of Jeremiah we read of God's new covenant with his people.

I shall set my law within them, writing it on their hearts; I shall be their God, and they will be my people. No longer need they teach one another, neighbour or brother, to know the Lord; all of them, high and low alike, will know me, says the Lord, for I shall forgive them their wrongdoing, and their sin I shall call to mind no more. (Jer. 31:33–4)

This passage was of particular significance to me when I moved after thirteen and a half years of inner city ministry to a suburban parish with a long tradition of able and distinguished clergy. The particular stress that each person, regardless of social standing, would learn to know God for themselves was especially significant. Maybe the main thrust of my own ministry in this place would be to emphasise our personal relationship with God and openness to him. For God's promise was not just for forgiveness – 'I will remember their sin no more' (Jer. 31:34 RSV) – but also for knowledge – 'all . . . will know me' for themselves.

But the context of this new personal relationship is in the contrast between the old and new covenants. A covenant is a mutual agreement between the two parties that remains in force only so long as both parties abide by its terms. The old covenant between God and his people had been annulled by Israel's disobedience. King Josiah had sought to reform matters but the reformation was ineffective. It dealt with external organisation. What was required was inward change, what Jeremiah called 'a circumcision of the heart' (Jer. 4:4). Religion must be internalised and spiritualised. Jeremiah knew from his own experience of communion with God that such experience could belong to everyone in Israel. Had not Moses exclaimed, 'I wish that all the Lord's people were prophets' (Num. 11:29).

But such a change could only come by a deep work in people's lives. 'I shall set my law within them, writing it on their hearts!' For the Jew the heart was not just a biological organ. It was the centre of a person's self-consciousness, the seat of his or her mind and will. Nothing less than a deep transformation would be necessary for the new covenant.

That was exactly how the prophet Ezekiel expressed God's purpose:

> I shall sprinkle pure water over you, and you will be purified from everything that defiles you . . . I shall give you a new heart and put a new spirit within you. I shall remove the heart of stone from your body and give you a heart of flesh. (Ezek. 36:25a, 26)

God's plan is to give them a new heart, a disposition and will responsive to his requirements. The hardness of their stony heart will be transformed into the sensitiveness of a heart of flesh. He will do yet more. His gift of a new spirit will enable them to render the obedience that is his due (Ezek. 36:27).

Phrases like 'born anew' and 'a new creation' were not then in use but this is precisely what the prophets had in mind. Our will becomes one with God's will and our meat and drink is to do his will. And we do so in grateful response to what a forgiving God has done for us.

For St Paul this new covenant is wrought by God in Christ. 'For anyone united to Christ, there is a new creation, the old order has gone; a new order has already begun. All this has been the work of God. He has reconciled us to himself through Christ' (2 Cor. 5:17, 18). In him then we have been made new, we are a new creation.

Yet this new creation needs continual affirmation and renewal. We need to become what we are. 'Do not lie to one another', St Paul exhorts the Colossians, reminding them who they are in Christ. 'Do not lie to one another, now that you have discarded the old human nature and the conduct that goes with it, and have put on the new nature which is constantly being renewed in the image of its Creator and brought to know God' (Col. 3:9, 10). The new heart that God has given us in Christ, the new being we have become in him needs constant cleansing and healing so that we can live as befits God's people in 'compassion, kindness, humility, gentleness and patience'.

The ministry of inner healing is one of the ways God enables

us to live out the new life we receive in Christ. Held back by
the wounds of the past, we need the liberating work of the
Spirit in our innermost being to set us free to become what
God has always intended for us.

I discovered an aspect of that in my own life through walking
the Three Peaks of Yorkshire. Penyghent (2,273 feet), Whern-
side (2,414) and Ingleborough (2,313) form the peaks, and the
route beginning and ending at Horton-in-Ribblesdale takes us
round them all. We ascend some 5,000 feet and cover twenty-
two and a half miles and it is a popular challenge for fell
runners and long distance walkers. I would never have seen
myself in either category. I had never attempted fell running
and long distance walking I felt was beyond me. But urged on
by my more energetic wife, I began to prepare for such a
possibility. I had taken up walking in my mid-thirties as a
regular exercise after conducting funerals of several men of the
same age, victims of coronary heart disease. But six or seven
or even ten miles was one thing – twenty-two and a half was
altogether different.

Nonetheless one damp August morning we got up especially
early, drove to Horton and by 7.40 a.m. Rosemary and I were
off. Nine eventful hours later we returned, the walk completed.
We had faced rain, very boggy conditions in parts and mist on
the top of Ingleborough which had meant taking our direction
from a compass bearing. But my wise guide saw me through.
And as I walked down into Horton, I felt both very tired and
very contented.

And then suddenly I remembered an incident from my childhood. In a vivid flashback I was at my preparatory school
standing talking to the headmaster. I was ten years old and
alongside me was my friend Taffinder. I had been picked to go
on a long distance walk. Taffinder hadn't. It was sixteen miles.
It sounded a very long distance. Taffinder was keen to go. I
wasn't particularly, so I offered to let him take my place. But
I had to have a reason. 'Well sir, you see I've got this poorly
leg at the moment and Taffinder's very keen to go, so can he
go in my place?'

The headmaster towered over me. A tall man, with a stern appearance, he seemed particularly forbidding that day. I cannot remember anything he said. But I do remember his look. It spoke volumes. 'You're feeble, Holmes, feeble!' His eyes seemed to pierce into my soul.

As I recalled the incident I realised why I had never believed I could walk any great distance. In a way I had been disabled by that memory. And only my wife's gentle encouragement had helped me overcome it. But as I did so I knew it had been God's work too. 'You see you can do it!' he seemed to be saying inside me as I walked the last two hundred yards to the café where the walk began and ended. You can do it.

So often the tape within says, 'You'll never manage it!' 'That's beyond you!' 'You're not worth that much!' 'You'll never be a success!' 'Don't try it, you'll only be disappointed!' And despite what we hear in church and know from our Bibles, we take more notice of the tape inside. So in one area of our life or another we are disabled, not physically, but emotionally and spiritually.

God wants to write on our hearts anew – with the law of his love. And part of that will involve wiping those unhelpful inner tapes clean and putting some new God-given messages on them. 'You can do it!' 'With my help, it is within your reach.' 'I created you, I died for you, I love you eternally – you're worth that much!' 'In me you can achieve what you're aiming for.' 'Trust me and I won't let you down.'

As bit by bit we know his healing within, our confidence grows as well. In our acknowledged weakness we begin to grow stronger, as God works in our hearts and restores us to his image.

As you have read this chapter, you may be aware of inner hurts that still sting and disable. Painful memories may have resurfaced. Bring them to God. Share them with someone who will be able to help. Seek God's healing and wholeness. May Jesus the wounded healer touch you with his love and set you free.

5

Stressed

Walking the Three Peaks of Yorkshire became a regular part of our lives. For several years we completed the walk each year. It was never easy, but always worthwhile. I particularly remember a winter circuit of the walk. It was a brilliantly clear, very cold day and the views from the top of Ingleborough were breathtaking.

But it was completing the walk for the first time that August day that opened a new world for me. It gave me the confidence to walk distances I had felt were quite beyond me. Nowadays I expect to complete the long distance walks I set out on, whether they are ten, fifteen or thirty miles or very occasionally even longer. Long distance walking has become an important recreation and the source of much enjoyment.

Yet walking isn't always easy. Sometimes it is really hard. I may get injured and have to take the short way home. I am often tired. Occasionally I get really despondent as the weather deteriorates and the end of the walk seems as far away as ever. It is for times like this that the badge we used to have on the rucksack seemed so appropriate, 'Keep me going, Lord.'

So, too, for our lives. Through new life in Christ and the healing of some of those inner wounds we can face life's challenges with new confidence and find at times real satisfaction. But that does not exempt us from problems or difficulties. We will face stress of one kind or another. Christians don't have a magic wand that exempts us from it.

I have often enjoyed singing the famous J. G. Whittier hymn, 'Dear Lord and Father of Mankind' and the verse

Drop thy still dews of quietness,
till all our strivings cease,
take from our souls the strain and stress,
and let our ordered lives confess
the beauty of thy peace.

It well expresses that desire God gives us for inner peace that grows out of a still centre at the heart of our being. But is it right to ask God to 'take from our souls the strain and stress'? Strain maybe – that sense of being unduly taut or tense. But stress is something we have to face and handle – and it will come to us as surely as it came to Jesus.

That's the standpoint of Dr Marjory Foyle in her useful book *Honourably Wounded* on stress among Christian workers. She has a special concern for missionaries. She recognises that within Christian circles,

There is a vocal minority that say Christians should not feel stressed. To feel so, they claim, indicates lack of faith or some deficit in relationship to God. For them, teaching about stress is irrelevant. What missionaries need is to be more spiritual, then the problems will automatically disappear.[1]

But neither the Scriptures nor an elementary knowledge of psychology can support such a view.

In John 16:33 Jesus warns his followers, 'In the world you will have trouble' (JB). The word translated 'trouble' is also used for anguish, persecution, suffering, distress and tribulation. In fact in the Amplified New Testament the verse reads, 'In the world you have tribulations and trials and distress and frustration!' Jesus is very plain about the cost of discipleship. 'If they persecuted me, they will also persecute you' (John 15:20). He realises the great pressure these difficulties will put on his followers. 'I have told you all this to guard you against the breakdown of your faith' (John 16:1). He wants to prepare his disciples for what they will face but he does so in a positive way. 'In the world you will have suffering. But take heart! I have conquered the world' (John 16:33). The stresses they will know can be the doorway to a new deeper awareness of Jesus' ruling presence with them.

That was Paul's experience. Trouble he knew in plenty. Anguish, persecution, suffering, distress and tribulation – he was familiar with them all. But in them he had known God's power to help.

> We are in difficulties on all sides, but never cornered; we see no answer to our problems, but never despair; we have been persecuted, but never deserted; knocked down, but never killed; always, wherever we may be, we carry with us in our body the death of Jesus, so that the life of Jesus, too, may always be seen in our body. (2 Cor. 4:8–10 JB)

The letter of James encourages a positive attitude to stress too. Written to Christian Jews probably scattered by persecution it begins: 'When all kinds of trials and temptations crowd into your lives, my brothers, don't resent them as intruders, but welcome them as friends! Realise that they come to test your faith and to produce in you the quality of endurance' (Jas. 1:2–3 J. B. Phillips). Such words were probably more easily composed at a distance – in time or place – from the particular trouble. And stresses, particularly great ones, hardly appear friendly when one is in the midst of them.

Yet psychology as well as the teaching of the New Testament does encourage us to recognise that stress can be useful for us. Dr Foyle, an experienced psychiatrist, writes:

> Stress alerts us to the need for constructive action. For example, when babies feel hunger, they experience an unpleasant inner sensation, rather like the sinking feeling of anxiety. This makes them cry, alerting the mother, who may be busy elsewhere. Young children going to school for the first time may look pale and not want to eat breakfast. As the school gates loom up the hand begins to tremble, and the child looks even more apprehensive. Similarly, new missionaries

sitting in the departure lounge or driving up the road to the new location usually feel nervous. The pulse rate rises, and thinking becomes apprehensive – 'Will it all be OK? How am I going to fit in? Will they like me?' Reactions of this kind are normal and helpful. They indicate that the body is being prepared for action. Chemicals and hormones stimulated by the stress are acting on certain parts of the nervous system, preparing the body for effective response.[2]

Dr Foyle then illustrates how this works in a typical situation for Christian work.

A missionary was sitting in a church vestry waiting to take part in a large service. She was feeling nervous and mentioned this to the senior pastor. In a somewhat severe tone of voice he said, 'But it's all of Him, isn't it?' Of course, it was, but God was using the normal human stress response to increase her effectiveness. The correct reaction to this type of stress experience is thankfulness to God for it. When we feel nervous before an event we pray a little more and increase our dependency on God for the work ahead. Our stress reaction has reminded us of our spiritual resources![3]

That understanding can apply to the stresses which affect us all. The death of someone close, changes in the family, injury, illness, redundancy, new work, a new home – all are causes of stress.

In September 1986 Rosemary was successfully interviewed for a new job, which would entail more responsibility in a new sphere of work. At the end of the same month we moved home, and early in October I became vicar of a new parish. During the same month Rosemary completed her work at her existing post and prepared for her new responsibilities. Then just before beginning them, her mother died suddenly. As the only child she took responsibility both for supporting her father and overseeing the arrangements.

In such a situation Rosemary inevitably felt stressed. Being aware of the various causes enabled her to acknowledge and handle the stress. She talked things over with me and others. She made allowances for herself, ensuring she got regular exercise and times of relaxation. She drew on the spiritual resources of her faith in prayer and worship. Like St Paul she acknowledged the need and found help, in the way that many do once they recognise the problem.

Writing to the Christians in Corinth St Paul lists the problems he has had to face. At the end of his list he concludes, 'Apart from these external things, there is the responsibility that weighs on me every day, my anxious concern for all the churches!' (2 Cor. 11:28). The nearest I have approached to Paul's great responsibilities was a four and a half year period as Rural Dean in a very urban deanery in South and West Leeds. There were fifteen parishes and twenty-five or so clergy and others in full-time church work for whom I had special care. But that concern did not fill me with the anxiety I experienced earlier in my ministry, as an ordinary parish priest returning home from holiday one year.

We had only been at the vicarage for a few minutes before the phone rang and my colleague asked if he could see me. We had not yet eaten after a long journey, so it was with that refreshment inside me I saw him a couple of hours later, sensing something bad. He wasn't given to ringing me in such a way. The bad news soon came out. His wife was having an affair with a married man in the congregation. The situation was very fraught. Not only were two families involved, but both couples affected by the relationship had key positions in the church. They were all closely associated with me and the policies I had pursued. Two marriages faced collapse, a gifted colleague's ministry was at the crossroads and the life of the local church could be mortally wounded.

The next few weeks and months were the most stressful of my ministry. I struggled with others to handle the situation. I made mistakes. The marriages ended in divorce eventually. Maybe that could have been avoided, or maybe the die was already cast. Strenuous efforts were made by various people to

help. My colleague moved on to a new situation, trying to
rescue his marriage and develop his ministry. His ministry survived and has prospered. So eventually did the life of the local
church, but only after great difficulty, much heart searching
and spiritual change that took many of us deeper in the Lord's
service.

For myself much of the time I felt I was just keeping my
head above water. For weeks I woke every day with a sense
of foreboding – a new experience for one basically optimistic.
I found the many difficult things I had to do and difficult
situations I had to face immeasurably draining. 'You've aged
ten years in three months', an older member of the congregation said to me one day towards the end of that time. I
certainly felt as though I had done – physically! But her comment was about an ageing in another sense. She believed I was
stronger, wiser, maturer. And doubtless I was. I had not seen
the troubles as 'friends' but certainly they had given me
'strength to endure' and I knew I had really developed both as
a person and as a priest. I felt I had entered more deeply into
the realities of human life and Christian service.

What were the key lessons I learnt in the midst of the trouble,
as I sought to serve others and keep my own life in some sort
of balance? What ways of handling stress did I learn at first
hand which have helped me face difficult situations since?

First I learnt the importance of acknowledging how I was
really feeling, admitting the pressure I felt under and the various emotions that were a part of it. It is an obvious lesson and
yet so often one which we are slow to put into practice. 'How
are you?' we're asked. 'Oh fine', we say, without a second
thought. Whereas in fact we feel and are far from fine. But we
swallow our feelings, or suppress them in one way or another
rather than admit to them. I learnt the importance of facing
them. Facing the fear. Would I be able to see this situation
through? Would the health of the church survive? Was my own
ministry in this parish mortally wounded? As I admitted the
questions the fear was giving rise to, they began to lose their
power. Gerard Hughes has said,

Fear like guilt is a healthy human reaction to danger, but if we refuse to face the fear, we cannot discover the danger which is threatening. If we refuse to face the fear, the fear may become a ruthless tyrant pervading and poisoning every aspect of our lives. Once faced, the fears often turn out to be illusory.[4]

Fr Hughes goes on to describe how this proved true for someone he calls 'Tom'. Through a dream Tom began to look at some of the fears in his own life. Some he found had vanished, while others turned out to be sources of strength. Fr Hughes comments,

One of the most constant refrains in the Old Testament and in the New is 'Do not be afraid'. God, in Christ, has overcome all the powers of evil and destruction. God is the God of surprises who can turn even the evil we have done, and the evil done to us, into the very means of our salvation.[5]

This was true of the anger I felt. Oh, I recognised my own fallibility. It was only too apparent every day and I was frustrated I had not foreseen the problem. But the affair and all the havoc it caused to so many was the last thing I had wanted. And I realised beneath my periodic sense of frustration and despair there was a real anger. This had to be admitted, so that it could be handled creatively, not destructively.

Robert Warren in *On the Anvil* shares the importance of learning the same lesson.

At the emotional level I have found great value in learning to harness anger rather than suppress it. I now see anger as energy for life if it is well used. So, if something goes wrong, or I feel put on by others, or some other pressure begins to tell, I resist the temptation to be 'noble' and suppress my feelings. Rather I seek to look at them, own them, and harness them to dealing with the problem. Anger can be very creative. Indeed, anger is emotional fire. In its raw and uncontrolled state it can do enormous harm. When harnessed, it is one of the most powerful, creative and essential forces known to man. We depend on fire for the warmth of our homes, for virtually all means of transport, and for light. Anger too can generate compassion, provide us with the motive power for change, and throw great light on the path ahead. Thus it gives the motivation to confront a problem that has been accepted until now. The result can be a permanent improvement: as long, of course, as Paul's words are heeded – 'Be angry but do not sin' (Eph. 4:26). Anger must be used creatively rather than destructively.[6]

Facing my feelings, admitting them rather than denying them or suppressing them was the first lesson I learnt in the midst of the trouble I faced.

Secondly I learnt to share my feelings. To express them to another and to talk them over. My wife Rosemary who had been called into Christian service with me, in fact before me, became my counsellor as well as my partner. We talked long and often, needing time alone to do so, most easily found away from the pressure of a busy vicarage.

Of course, not just anyone would do. When some people ask us 'How are you?' to burden them with a full answer would neither help them nor do anything for us. The need for good counsel, the listening ear of someone wise and understanding was so vital. I found it as many can do in their marriage partner. But I found valuable help in others too.

I have had a spiritual director from the time of being ordained. He was a great help. He was an older more experienced priest who drew from the depths of his own compassion and common sense the capacity to help me know deep within the strength of wise loving support. 'Help to carry one another's burdens, and in this way you will obey the law of Christ', St Paul said to the Galatians (6:2 GNB) and I knew that help indeed.

The little girl was carrying her brother along the Glasgow street. He had hurt himself and his sister was taking him home.

But she was making very slow progress, since she was only a little bigger than he was. Watching the scene, a bystander called to the girl warmly, 'You've got a real burden there!' 'He's no burden', the girl replied. 'He's my brother.' It was that quality of loving support I found as I shared with others.

I learnt thirdly as I sought to cope with the problem to be gentle with myself. To make allowances physically for the pressure I was under emotionally. Exercise seemed particularly important and some of my most useful conversations with Rosemary at this time came during long walks in the Yorkshire Dales or Moors. But often a brief walk from home would help relieve the pressure and enable me to think more clearly.

Relaxation was vital too, giving not just physical refreshment but that inner renewal that can flow from a good film, or play or even a meal. All this helped restore my energy which seemed to be so easily drained by the difficult meetings and decisions I was regularly faced with, for a while without an obvious resolution in sight.

John Sanford, the priest and psychologist, tells the story of a musician he was seeking to help who was in a terrible depression.

No amount of psychology or prayer seemed to help. He was driving home one day when he had a flat tyre. He got out of the car and inspected the depressing situation, went to the trunk and fumbled around for the jack. He could not remember when he had last changed a tyre and had all but forgotten how to use the tools. He worked for over an hour changing the tyre, and when he had finished he was completely out of his depression. He could not understand it, but he felt like a new man.

Later he had a dream of a large, strong black man with tools in his hands. Taking the cue from the dream he purchased some tools, followed some impulses in himself he had submerged, and proceeded to remodel part of his house. His music became meaningful again; the work with the tools brought him renewing energy that revitalised, rather than detracted from, his main occupation.[7]

The musician's new recreation helped recreate him. Each of us will find in our own way and from our own interests the particular ways we can be restored and renewed as we face the emotional drain of stress.

Through all the particular time of difficulty I faced, as I acknowledged the way I felt and shared it with others who were wise and understanding and sought to compensate in recreation and relaxation for the emotional drain, I was taken deeper into the reality of God. He was present in the whole process I have just described. In my honest admission of just how I was and how I felt. In the wise and loving meetings – of silence as well as words – as I shared my need with others. In my various recreative activities as I listened to my body and took greater care of it.

He was present each morning, as I opened my eyes and suddenly realised again the measure of what lay ahead. To handle my despondency and remind myself just who I am and whose I am I would pray, 'You are my Father and I am your son', 'You are my God and I am your child'. For weeks, before getting out of bed I began each day with those words on my lips. They put things in true perspective, for I learnt with and through all the other lessons, to rely on God in a deeper way than ever before and to hold on to him.

The Psalms became especially significant for me. I used them as the basis for my daily time of quiet and started underlining words and phrases that held particular meaning.

'For the ruin of the poor, for the groans of the needy,
now I will arise,' says the Lord,
'I will place him in the safety for which he longs.'

Even though I walk through a valley dark as death.
I fear no evil, for thou art with me . . .

Wait for the Lord; be strong, take courage,
    and wait for the Lord.

The Lord will give strength to his people;
the Lord will bless his people with peace.

But, Lord, I put my trust in thee
    I say, 'Thou art my God.'
    My fortunes are in thy hand.

Unfailing love enfolds him who trusts in the Lord.
        (Pss. 12:5, 23:4, 27:14, 29:11, 31:14, 32:10 NEB)

I attended a confirmation service at which Bishop David
Young preached on the words from Psalm 27:1, 'The Lord is
the stronghold of my life'. He said this reminded us not just
that we can take strong hold of God, but that he has strong
hold of us. And that seemed above all what God was showing
me, as he deepened my relationship with him. 'Anxious
thoughts may fill my heart, but thy presence is my joy and my
consolation' (Ps. 94:19).

'Abba' was the word on Jesus' lips when he faced his own
supreme time of trial in Gethsemene. Abba, dear Father,
Daddy, maybe even Dada. Joachim Jeremias comments,

It was something new, something unique and unheard of,
that Jesus dared to take this step and to speak with God as
a child speaks with his father, simply, intimately, securely.
There is no doubt that the Abba which Jesus uses to address
God reveals the very basis of his communion with God.

And of ours too. 'When you pray, say "Father" ' (Luke
11:2). Jesus invites us to approach God with the same sim-
plicity, intimacy and security.

St Paul sees this as the product of the Spirit's work in our
lives.

All who follow the leading of God's Spirit are God's own

sons. Nor are you meant to relapse into the old slavish attitude of fear – you have been adopted into the very family circle of God and you can say with a full heart, 'Father, my Father'. (Rom. 8:14 J. B. Phillips)

So with a full heart I did say 'Abba, Father' and found my place more deeply than ever before in his love, weak as I was.

This chapter is entitled 'Stressed'. You may be under particular stress at the moment. Face your feelings. Share them with someone you can trust who will listen and care and maybe offer wise counsel. Look after yourself. Compensate for your loss of energy with recreation and relaxation. And hold on to God, as he holds on to you. Affirm your relationship with him. Rely on him. He loves you. He cares for you.

The Lord who created you says, 'Do not be afraid – I will
    save you.
I have called you by name – you are mine.
When you pass through deep waters, I will be with you;
    your troubles will not overwhelm you.
When you pass through fire, you will not be burnt;
    the hard trials that come will not hurt you.
For I am the Lord your God,
    the holy God of Israel, who saves you.'
                                (Isa. 43:1–3 GNB)

The buck stops here!

It's a good few years ago now, but they still remember it. The vicar caused a real stir. It was the noticeboard that did it – the noticeboard the vicar put outside the parish church of Otley, the market town in Lower Wharfedale. Its message in gold lettering was unmistakeable.

THIS CHURCH IS FOR SINNERS ONLY

Of course the vicar was only wanting to encourage the notion that anyone and everyone was welcome at church. But it drew considerable criticism. A group of church people asked him to remove it. 'It's a bit strong, isn't it? Surely it should say, "This church *welcomes* sinners." That would be alright, but to assume *everyone* is a sinner . . .'

But we are.'All have sinned and fall short of the glory of God' (Rom. 3:23 RSV). If we need to acknowledge to God our weakness, the weakness of suffering, hurt, anguish, stress, we need to own too the weakness of our sin. This is not just a theological truth, but a fact of human experience. Bishop John Robinson said that all people 'find themselves born into an historical order where sin is there before them, dragging them down' and Professor Herbert Butterfield concluded, 'What history does is to uncover Man's universal sin.'

Yet admitting our *own* sin is sometimes more difficult. The vicar's poster in Otley became a major talking point. In the barber shop it was roundly discussed. A minister from a neighbouring parish was having his hair cut. He defended his colleague, 'Surely it says in the Prayer Book confession in Evening Prayer, "We have erred and strayed from thy ways like lost sheep, and there is no health in us".' The hairdresser, a regular attender, made a terse response, 'I never say it!' Sin was somebody else's problem, not his. In the Garden of Eden the man blamed the woman. The woman blamed the serpent. And the serpent hadn't a leg to stand on. We are good at passing the buck.

President Truman had a simple sign on his desk. It read, 'The buck stops here.' The machinery of government was a complicated one, but he knew his ultimate responsibility. It is as true for us. Our own lives are complex, and various influences, physical changes, events and experiences make for the person we are. But we cannot grow in the Christian life until we are willing to take responsibility for our own sinful attitudes and actions, even under provocation.

An experienced priest I knew was particularly tired. He had married in his fifties, and then his wife had given birth to twin boys. His wife coped well, but family life was a shock to the priest's system. Holy Week had always been a busy time, but that year the teething problems of the twins made it almost impossible! He celebrated the new life of Easter Day, feeling half-dead. His twin sons were livelier in church, too lively for one of the elderly members of his congregation. She sharply criticised the priest for the noise the boys had made. It was the last straw – and all the sleepless nights, strain and hard work of the previous days gave way to a violent verbal outburst. Several people left the church upset that day, including the priest. His reaction had been understandable, but he knew it was wrong. As he realised, we have to take responsibility for our actions whatever the context. I learnt the same lesson myself early in my ministry dealing with a particularly awkward and difficult teenager in the youth club. Yet another stupid action from the boy had provoked me, and my frustration overflowed in a torrent of verbal criticism that went beyond appropriate correction. My words were damaging and it took a long time to repair them.

In baptism we are urged to 'fight valiantly under the banner
of Christ against sin, the world and the devil'. To engage in
this spiritual warfare is an inevitable consequence of seeking
to follow Christ. I've been much aware of this spiritual conflict
as a bishop's advisor for the ministry of deliverance in my own
diocese.

But so often the enemy is in fact within us, and while we
can point one finger at others, unfailingly three fingers point
back to ourselves.

That was the conclusion writer and explorer Laurens van der
Post reached while in a Japanese prisoner of war camp in Java.

I had been drawn steadily over the years to a conclusion
which has become almost a major article of faith. Men, I
believed, were their own greatest villain – they themselves
were the flies in their own ointment. Villains undoubtedly
do exist in the wide world without. But they do so, in a
mysterious and significant state of inter-dependence with the
profoundest failures and inadequacies in ourselves and our
attitudes to life. It is almost as if the villain without is a
Siamese twin of all that is wrong within ourselves. The only
sure way to rid life of villains, I believed, after years of
thinking about it in prison, was to rid ourselves first of the
villain within our own individual and native collective con-
texts. If we could take care of the measure of the failures in
ourselves, I was certain that the world on the whole would
ultimately take better care of itself.[1]

Jesus took a sombre view of what is inside us: 'From inside,
from the human heart, come evil thoughts, acts of fornication,
theft, murder, adultery, greed, and malice; fraud, indecency,
envy, slander, arrogance, and folly; all these evil things come
from within, and they are what defile a person' (Mark 7:21–3).

Is it any wonder then that the first word on Jesus' lips in
Matthew's summary of his message is 'Repent'! 'Repent, for
the kingdom of heaven is upon you' (Matt. 4:17). Turn from
your sins and come back to God. And it's the first word on

Peter's lips too, when the crowds on the day of Pentecost ask him how they can respond to his message, 'Repent and be baptized, every one of you, in the name of Jesus the Messiah' (Acts 2:38).

Yet this invitation is good news. Repentance is good for us and brings us good. And when so many started to repent and believe in the good news, they themselves became good news.

> One and all they kept up their daily attendance at the temple, and, breaking bread in their homes, they shared their meals with unaffected joy, as they praised God and enjoyed the favour of the whole people. And day by day the Lord added new converts to their number. (Acts 2:46–7)

Repentance is not about wallowing in one's sin, but recognising the deadness within us and opening ourselves to new life. Repentance is a bold life-affirming response to God's love. It needs a basic honesty on our part, of course, but the honest recognition of weakness can open the door to new joy and vitality. As Bishop John V. Taylor said to students of Oxford University during a mission there in 1986:

> Repentance doesn't mean sackcloth and ashes and the beating of breasts. It may mean tears, but they will be of joy and relief as much as of sorrow. Repentance means turning so as to face in another direction. Repentance will be an honest recognition of one's past choices of death rather than life and a resolve to open oneself towards the renewal of awareness and response.[2]

In the Old Testament we hear of the challenge drawn up by Moses to be given to the Israelites at the ancient fortress of Shechem after their conquest and occupation of Palestine. They were presented with a simple choice, one which faces us all: 'Today I offer you the choice of life and good, or death and evil . . . Choose life and you and your descendants will live' (Deut. 30:15, 19).

C. S. Lewis became aware of the same choice in his own life as he recounts in his autobiography *Surprised by Joy*:

The odd thing was that before God closed in on me, I was in fact offered what now appears a moment of wholly free choice. In a sense, I was going up Headington Hill on the top of a bus. Without words and (I think) almost without images, a fact about myself was somehow presented to me. I became aware that I was holding something at bay, or shutting something out. Or, if you like, that I was wearing some stiff clothing, like corsets, or even a suit of armour, as if I were a lobster. I felt myself being, there and then, given a free choice. I could open the door or keep it shut; I could unbuckle the armour or keep it on. Neither choice was presented as a duty; no threat or promise was attached to either, though I knew that to open the door or to take off the corset meant the incalculable. The choice appeared to be momentous, but it was also strangely unemotional. I was moved by no desires or fears. In a sense I was not moved by anything. I chose to open, to unbuckle, to loosen the rein.[3]

That choice was of critical importance for C. S. Lewis, and all his subsequent life was affected by it. We may have known such vital choices in our own lives too. Choices which in C. S. Lewis' words, are 'momentous' affecting the whole course of life for us.

Yet in another sense we face such choices as a regular feature of our lives as Christians, not as momentous maybe, but just as real. Our choice is whether to admit the weakness, deadness within us and accept the invitation to receive afresh the life and strength of Christ. The letter to the Hebrews speaks of the sin 'which clings so closely' (Heb. 12:1) and it is so often the habitual sin that dogs our lives and deadens our spirit. P. T. Forsyth said, 'It is not the sins that damn but the sin into which sins settle down'. It is those persistent failures in love, self-control, purity which so often spoil Christ's work in us – and if they seem so slight in comparison with some other sin, they nonetheless can drag us low.

Fr Michel Quoist expresses clearly the prayer of a man hounded by small temptations that threaten to engulf him:

I'm at the end of my tether, Lord
I am shattered,
I am broken,
Since this morning I have been struggling to escape
    temptation,
  which, now subtle, now persuasive, now tender, now
  sensuous, dances before me like a glamour girl at a fair.
I don't know what to do,
I don't know where to go.
It spies on me, follows me, engulfs me.
When I leave a room I find it seated and waiting for me in
    the next.
I don't know where I stand, Lord,
I don't know whether or not I want this sin that beckons
    me.
I no longer know whether I pursue it or am pursued.
I am dizzy, and the void draws me as it draws the rash
    mountaineer
  who can neither advance nor retreat.
Lord, Lord, help me.

Son, I am here.
I haven't left you.
How weak is your faith!

You are too proud.
You still rely on yourself.
If you want to surmount all temptations, without falling or
    weakening, calm and serene,
You must surrender yourself to me.
You must realize that you are neither big enough nor
    strong enough,

You must let yourself be guided like a child . . .
Come, give me your hand, and do not fear.
If there is mud, I will carry you in my arms.[4]

There are times in all our lives when we need to hear those
words of reassurance. Times when our weakness becomes so
obvious, our vulnerability to temptation so low, and sin itself
seems to be getting the upper hand. Times when we wonder if
we are beyond hope.

Pope John XXIII used to visit the prisoners in Regina Caeli,
the Roman prison, and the prisoners were encouraged by his
presence. Among them were two convicted murderers. One of
them approached him and asked, 'Are your words of hope also
meant for a great sinner like me?' Pope John XXIII replied
simply by opening his arms and embracing him.[5]

So God the Father responds to the returning prodigal son in
all of us, running to meet us, flinging his arms round us and
embracing us with his love (Luke 15:20). The welcoming,
cleansing forgiveness of God is such good news.

And life without it is black. Before I was ordained, I worked
for a time at a psychiatric hospital. A man in one ward there
walked around all day saying 'No! No! No!' I enquired about
him. Apparently many years before he had done something for
which he could not forgive himself and it had literally turned
his mind.

I wanted to speak to him, communicate with him, but sadly
he was beyond communication. I wanted to say to him, 'Whatever you've done, it can be forgiven! To your No, there is a
Yes from God. There is forgiveness for the sins of the past.
There is new life for the future.'

I found the new life of God's forgiveness myself when I made
my first confession. I was in my second year at university. Only
a couple of weeks earlier the penny dropped and I had realised
for the first time what Christ had done for me. It was the
culmination of months of reflection and discussion and the
prayers of others unbeknown to me then. But the moment of
clear understanding and simple surrender came at the end of

an ordinary evening service in the Hostel of the Resurrection in Leeds. We had just sung the hymn 'When I survey the wondrous Cross' and its last two verses had found their way to my heart:

> See from his head, his hands and feet
> sorrow and love flow mingling down;
> did e'er such love and sorrow meet,
> or thorns compose so rich a crown?

> Were the whole realm of nature mine,
> that were an offering far too small;
> love so amazing, so divine,
> demands my soul, my life, my all.

Those who had most clearly commended Christ to me were Anglican ordinands, from a predominantly Anglo-Catholic background. I was encouraged to make a clear confession of my sin to God before a priest, to make a clean breast of it all for a fresh start in my life. I prepared for the confession fastidiously, almost obsessively. There was a lot to confess! But the wise priest who guided me told me to concentrate on the main things that had been wrong, where my selfishness had taken greatest root. I found making the confession about the most humiliating thing I had ever done, not just acknowledging to God but before someone else how I had indeed 'erred and strayed from thy ways like (a) lost sheep', following too much 'the devices and desires of my own heart.' But the assurance of forgiveness in the absolution brought the greatest sense of relief and freedom I had known in my life up to then. As the priest bade me, 'The Lord has put away your sin. Go in peace and pray for me, a sinner', I felt a great burden lifted off me. I was clean, free, forgiven.

I have made a regular practice of making a private confession since and have encouraged others to do so. I know full well it is God alone who forgives and that Christ has won our forgiveness once for all on the Cross. I know that many Christians find their own confession of sin to God in their private prayers and public worship a sufficient way of knowing his forgiveness. But the letter of James urges us, 'Therefore confess your sins to one another, and pray for one another, that you may be healed' (Jas. 5:16). For some there is real benefit in sharing with another in the Lord's presence the burden of sin. I have found evangelical Christians as well as Catholics who see that need. Certainly the Book of Common Prayer recognises it. In the words of the Exhortation given by the minister:

> If there be any of you who cannot quiet his own conscience, but requireth further comfort or counsel, let him come to me, or to some other discreet and learned Minister of God's Word, and open his grief, that by the Ministry of God's holy Word he may receive the benefit of absolution together with ghostly counsel and advice, to the quieting of his conscience, and avoiding of all scruple and doubtfulness.

Florrie could not quiet her own conscience. After years away from God in her values and lifestyle, she wanted to make her peace with God in the only way she knew how: to make a confession to God before a priest. So on my first visit to her home she asked to do so there and then. I don't know who was more moved, myself or Florrie. As she shared her sin and heard Christ's royal word of forgiveness, she wept with joy and relief. I wept with her. I'm sure there was joy in heaven too.

For Marlene her awareness of God's forgiveness came in an ordinary church service. She had a very stormy marriage and had just gone through one of her periodic separations. Wrestling with her own love for her husband and her hurt at his periodic lapses, she had come to church in a very needy state. During the service she found strength to forgive her husband, as she found forgiveness herself. She said afterwards, 'I feel clean, really clean.'

So often our own forgiveness is linked with forgiveness for others. As Jesus taught us to pray, 'forgive us our sins, for we too forgive all who have done us wrong' (Luke 11:14). Some translations of the version of the Lord's Prayer in St Matthew's Gospel express that phrase rather differently, 'forgive us our debts, as we also have forgiven our debtors' (Matt. 6:12 RSV, AV). Dr Foyle explains the significance of these words to her,

> What we are doing when we forgive others is forgiving their debt to us. It is not a blotting out, the end result being as if the event had never happened. It did happen, and cannot be erased. People may have hurt us, taken something away from us, or failed to provide what they should have done. This means they owe us a debt, and it is the debt we forgive.[6]

Perhaps we were not loved as children and received brutality. Forgiving such a debt is healing for it is voluntary – we choose to forgive. This makes us masters of the situation, not helpless victims, leading to increased maturity.

Laurens van der Post saw this principle at work in his three and a half years in a Japanese POW camp.

> It was amazing how often and how many of my men would confess to me, after some Japanese excess worse than usual, that for the first time in their lives they had realized the truth, and the dynamic liberating power of the first of the Crucifixion utterances: 'Forgive them for they know not what they do'.
>
> I found that the moment they grasped this fundamental fact of our prison situation, forgiveness became not a product of an act of will or of personal virtue even, but an automatic and all-compelling consequence of a law of under-standing . . . The tables of the spirit would be strangely and promptly turned and we would find ourselves without self-pity of any kind, feeling deeply sorry for the Japanese as if we were the free men and they the prisoners – men held in some profound oubliette of their own minds.[7]

Forgiveness, van der Post concluded from his prison experi-ence, was not just a theological maxim, but a law of the human spirit. 'If one broke this law of forgiveness, one inflicted a mortal wound on one's spirit and became once again a member of the chain gang of mere cause and effect from which life has laboured so long and painfully to escape'. As Jesus said, 'When you stand praying, if you have a grievance against anyone, forgive him, so that your Father in heaven may forgive you the wrongs you have done' (Mark 11:25). That's the way of maturity and freedom. Our acts of forgiveness enable the healing Holy Spirit to flow more freely through our lives, for our own good and others. But time and again we rub up against our own need for forgiveness.

Four years ago I went on a residential retreat led by Canon Peter Peterken from Derby diocese. It was held in the Yorkshire Wolds at Lamplugh House, Thwing. Fr Peterken is an able retreat conductor. In his addresses, leading of prayer and worship, in his counsel and personal ministry he enables the retreatants to find afresh in the silence Christ's word and power.

I was specially aware of Christ's power in this retreat following an address on forgiveness. Fr Peterken took the call of Isaiah in chapter 6 as the basis of his addresses. Each time we met we looked at some theme suggested by the passage: seeing God (v. 1), recognising his holiness (v. 3), knowing our sin and our forgiveness (vv. 5–7), knowing his call (v. 8) and going for him, 'Here I am! Send me' (v. 9).

In the third address we were encouraged to reflect on our sin. 'I am lost; for I am a man of unclean lips, and I dwell in the midst of a people of unclean lips' (v. 5 RSV). Fr Peterken did not speak for long, but his talk went to the heart of the matter.

So many within the church enjoy the blessings of God but with little real desire to be changed, to be made holy . . . forms of confession in our liturgies often slip too easily off the tongue . . . We need to make repentance a reality by regular specific self-examination. Jesus came not only to blot out our sin but also to make us holy, to redeem us from sin and make us new.

We were challenged to look afresh at our relationship with other people and with God. We were invited to turn our self-examination into a practical exercise, noting down on a piece of paper any particular sin or sins that clung so closely. Yet we were urged to remember that self-examination was not a heavy thing but something joyful, for 'when we confess our sins, we ought to praise God' (St Augustine) for all that he's forgiven us in his great mercy.

My own self-examination did not take long. My particular failings stared me in the face. One I was especially aware of: I had been struggling with it particularly before the retreat.

The following morning we gathered for the Eucharist. We brought our pieces of paper with us. Though the exercise had been entirely voluntary, there were many pieces of paper put in the bowl in the middle of the chapel. We were invited to renew our baptismal vows.

> I turn to Christ
> I repent of my sins
> I renounce evil

Then the absolution pronounced, the papers were burnt. 'As far as the east is from the west; so far has he set our sins from us' (Ps. 103:12 ASB Psalter).

But this was no mere ritual. We knew God's cleansing forgiveness afresh. The chain of sin had been broken again in our lives. 'If then the Son sets you free, you will indeed be free' (John 8:36). We were free. For myself at least I knew an important step forward in my life as a Christian then. Acknowledging the weakness of my sin, I found even more God's power to save and help. I knew the fruits of that in the weeks that followed.

May I invite you to examine afresh your relationship with others and with God. Is there a particular sin (or sins) that clings so closely? Or do you feel broken by sin, a captive of sin? In Reading gaol Oscar Wilde wrote,

How else but through a broken heart
May the Lord Christ enter in?

Admit your sins to God. Write them down. Share them with
another if you feel the need to. Then come to the Lord. Know
he loves you and forgives you. If you've written your sin down,
now burn the paper. Receive his cleansing power. Open your
heart to his love. Find afresh his freedom. 'Go in peace. The
Lord has put away your sin. And pray for me, a sinner.'

Breakthrough

In the collect for the third Sunday after the Epiphany in the
Alternative Service Book we ask God to

> renew your people with heavenly grace
> and in all our weakness
> sustain us by your mighty power;
> through Jesus Christ our Lord.

That was very much the prayerful intention of those who
gathered at Duquesne University, Pittsburgh in Pennsylvania
in 1967 for a weekend of prayer and fasting to ask the grace
of the Holy Spirit.

Who were they? Young Roman Catholics. Students who at
a time of social and religious crises throughout their own
country and the world at large were finding increasingly that a
human solution was impossible. For the most part they were
members of the University already engaged in movements concerned with the liturgy, ecumenism, the struggle for civil rights,
and efforts in support of world peace. They were not inward-
looking Christians unconcerned for the world about them.
Rather they actively sought to live out their faith for a world
in need. Yet as Kevin and Dorothy Raneghan have said,

> they felt there was something lacking in their individual
> Christian lives. They couldn't quite put their finger on it, but
> somehow there was an emptiness, a lack of dynamism, a
> sapping of strength in their lives of prayer.[1]

They felt spiritually weak and they recognised why. 'It was as if their lives as Christians were too much their own creation, as if they were moving forward under their own power and of their own will. It seemed to them that the Christian life wasn't meant to be a purely human achievement'.

'When everything is crumbling, then one is facing reality', St Augustine said. That is what those young Roman Catholic Christians faced. And they committed themselves to a weekend of prayer because they had discovered what Abraham Lincoln knew: 'I have often been driven to my knees in prayer, because I had nowhere else to go'.

They had prepared for the weekend. They had read together St Paul's letters and the Acts of the Apostles and some of them had recited, every day for a year, the sequence from the Octave of Pentecost in their own liturgy, 'Come, Holy Spirit'. They had kept in their hearts that same yearning for a new Pentecost Pope John XXIII had prayed for on the eve of the Second Vatican Council, 'O Holy Spirit, renew your wonders in this our day, as by a new Pentecost'.

So they gathered for a weekend together to ask the Holy Spirit to come and renew the face of the Church and of the whole earth.

And what happened? Cardinal Suenens in his book *A New Pentecost* describes the first fruits of their prayer:

> The Spirit's response to them was an experience, over again, of what happened when the first disciples of the Lord were together in the upper room in Jerusalem. An amazing spiritual transformation took place in them. They spoke of a new awareness of the love of God such as they had not experienced before; of a desire to pray and glorify God; of an insatiable thirst for Scripture. Moreover they felt power within them to bear witness to the risen Jesus. They talked of a 'baptism in the Holy Spirit' and of charisms given to them similar to those of which we recall in the early Church. They did not consider this 'baptism in the Holy Spirit' as in any way a replacement of the sacraments of baptism and

confirmation. The key is to be found in the words of one of them: 'It seemed, rather, a kind of adult re-affirmation and renewal of these sacraments, an opening of ourselves to all their sacramental graces'.[2]

Many Christians over the last three decades especially have experienced what those young Roman Catholic students knew that weekend in 1967, a spiritual renewal. A rediscovery, after a recognition of weakness even emptiness in their Christian lives, of the power and vitality of God's Holy Spirit. Many Protestants, Anglicans and Roman Catholics throughout the world can share their own stories of spiritual breakthrough.

Cardinal Suenens speaks of his spiritual debt to this renewal in his own life. Many years a priest and bishop he knew well the work of the Holy Spirit in his life already. Yet as he wrote later,

I found that I believed in the action of the Holy Spirit, but in a limited sphere; in me the Spirit could not call forth from the organ all the melody he wished; some of the pipes did not function, because they had not been used. I could have discovered this without the Renewal. Anyone can read the Acts of the Apostles and letters of St Paul, and then, by way of contrast with what he sees in himself, make an examination of conscience. However, the Renewal enabled me to see the beginnings of the Church in a new light and gave me a living example of that same faith for which I shall always be grateful.

In asking a group of friends to pray for me, and in receiving their fraternal gesture of solidarity as they laid hands on me and prayed that I be more and more faithful to the Holy Spirit, I was carrying out, I reflected, St Paul's injunction to Timothy; 'That is why I am reminding you now to fan into a flame the gift that God gave you when I laid my hands on you. God's gift was not a spirit of timidity, but the Spirit of power, and love and self control' (2 Tim. 1:6–7).[3]

Cardinal Suenens saw himself like Timothy needing spiritual renewal.

We first encounter Timothy in the Acts of the Apostles. In Chapter 16 we read how Paul 'went on to Derbe and then to Lystra, where he found a disciple named Timothy, the son of a Jewish Christian mother and a gentile father'. Timothy came from good spiritual stock. 'I am reminded', Paul wrote to him later, 'of the sincerity of your faith, a faith which was alive in Lois your grandmother and Eunice your mother before you' (2 Tim. 1:5). Timothy is well spoken of by the believers, so Paul takes him with him to become his colleague and assistant, his protegé to whom Paul would later give responsibility in the church.

In his second letter to Timothy Paul writes to encourage him. He had earlier prayed for him with the laying on of hands, when Timothy had known the empowering of the Spirit. Now Paul urges him to rekindle the gift that God had given him, to stir into flame the gift of the Spirit (2 Tim. 1:6). But why does he need to exhort him to do that?

We don't know the reason precisely, but the letters do give us clues. Timothy was young and yet he had to exercise leadership and ministry among those who were older. Maybe he found it difficult to be balanced and fair. Moreover Timothy had health problems. 'In view of your frequent ailments take a little wine to help your digestion' (1 Tim. 5:23). Did Timothy have a 'timid tummy'? Did he have a rather nervous disposition? Certainly Timothy is urged not to be *ashamed* of the gospel, but to be *insistent* proclaiming the message 'and to do so in a *mature* and gentle way' (2 Tim. 1:8, 2 Tim. 4:2, 2 Tim. 2:22–5).

Faced by his responsibilities Timothy probably felt weak and lacking in confidence and Paul urged him to seek to be filled afresh with the Spirit of power, love and self-control.

There was a time in my own life and ministry when I felt like Timothy, very short of power and love. I was in my second year as vicar of St Luke's in inner city Leeds. That summer I had experienced two significant pastoral failures.

I had got to know a young man in his early twenties after he had tried to commit suicide. He had no one in the world. He had long lost contact with his family. We offered him the hospitality of our home whenever he wanted. He lived at the hotel he worked in, but most of his free time he spent with us. People at church got used to seeing him around. For a while everything was fine. 'Isn't this what it's all about?' I thought to myself one day. 'Offering love to the loveless!' But then the love started to run out. Neil continued to come to see us, but his visits became more and more burdensome. He always told the same story, like an old record getting stuck on the turntable. Then one day he disappeared. We never heard or saw him again. I was devastated. I knew he had realised he had out-stayed his welcome. Was this the love that 'bears all things, believes all things, hopes all things, endures all things'? (1 Cor. 13:17 RSV).

Then one of our neighbours tried to take her life. A mother of three small children in a difficult marriage, her suicide attempt was a cry for help. I heard it and visited her. I got to know her quite well. It was clear to me what Karen needed. She longed to know the love of God, that he accepted her and would help her. Of course, I offered that love to her in my visits, but I needed to express it, to put into words the faith I had which I believed she sought. I stood at the side of her bed in the hospital ward – tongue-tied. Somehow I could not convey to her what I knew she needed to hear. I asked the chaplain to do so instead. He did and led her to a living faith which changed her life.

Just what sort of a Christian minister was I? Weak in love. Not able to share my faith when I most needed to do so. I came from a family of business men. I had read eagerly Beveridge's book *Managing the Church* on the application of management by objectives to the daily life of the local church. But I knew good management alone could not bring life to an ailing church. More was needed, and I needed more. There was a big hole at the heart of my ministry. Neil and Karen had shown

me what I had known deep down for a while. I needed to know
more of God in my life.

W. A. Vissert 'Hooft, of the World Council of Churches,
has said:

> 'Be renewed' does not mean 'Get busy and find some differ-
> ent and better method of Christian action'. It means 'Expose
> yourself to the life-giving work of God'. Pray that he brings
> dry bones to life – expect great things from him – and get
> ready to do what he commands.

That was what I needed, but how?

The year before, Rosemary and I had gone to a day conference on 'The Missing Dimension' at St Matthias Burley. The
conference was on the Holy Spirit. Maybe this was the missing
dimension. Pope Leo XIII way back in 1897 had thought so:
'Perhaps even today if we were to ask some Christians whether
they have received the Holy Spirit, they would answer like the
disciples St Paul met at Ephesus, "we had not even heard that
there was any such thing as the Holy Spirit".'

But I knew about the Holy Spirit. I knew the Holy Spirit
had been working in my life, at baptism, at confirmation, when
I'd come to a new deeper commitment while at university and
at ordination. I had preached on the Holy Spirit. I knew he
was the third person of the Trinity. I knew better than the
confused Japanese convert who had exclaimed, 'God the Father
I know, God the Son I know but who is this holy bird?'

But how much did I know? When I listened to the speakers
at the day conference I realised that there was a large gap in
my Christian experience. Brian Ellis, an evangelical Anglican
vicar in Leeds, spoke quietly and simply of the way the Holy
Spirit had helped renew his marriage and ministry. Brother
Jeremy from the Community of the Resurrection spoke
enthusiastically and humorously of the spiritual renewal breaking out in different parts of the worldwide church. And an
invitation was given to all of us, clergy and laity, to respond.
Many did.

I held back. Was it fear, fear of what others would say, other clergy especially? Or was it an instinct that Rosemary and I should move forward spiritually together? Maybe I needed to be more aware of my need.

Fifteen months later I was. The summer pastoral failures had seen to that. And the reading I had done during our holidays had reinforced my desire to know more of God in my life and ministry. So in September 1974 Rosemary and I attended a conference on the Holy Spirit at the Community of the Resurrection, Mirfield, just twelve miles away from where we lived. It was a joint Anglican-Roman Catholic Conference and had several distinguished speakers, though the names meant little to me then. It proved to be a turning-point for both of us.

For Rosemary first of all. During the final service of the conference she made a fresh surrender of her life to God. As she did so, she was aware of the Holy Spirit filling her with a new security and joy. I saw a change in her when she returned home.

I was not at the final service. I had parish commitments I needed to fulfil but the conference and Rosemary's experience spurred me on. A few days later I returned to Mirfield for a quiet day. During the day I asked two of the monks from the Community to pray for me. We met in the chapel of the Retreat House there. Without any emotional experience I knew the presence of God's Spirit in the quiet and sensed a new beginning in my life and ministry.

'The Holy Spirit praying in us heals and renews us at the very centre of our being, that is to say in our hearts'. These words from the agreed statement of Anglican-Orthodox dialogue express well what was happening to me: a renewal in the heart of my life and in my relationship with God. 'Through the Holy Spirit he has given us, God's love has flooded our hearts' (Rom. 5:5).

Of course this was no first encounter with the Spirit. This was a renewal. Yet it touched on the very basis of my life as a baptised Christian. Canon John Gunstone has said, 'Renewal begins in the Church when individual Anglicans begin to know by personal experience as well as by intellectual conviction, what it means to be baptised' (for 'Anglicans' we can read all Christians).

The Holy Spirit enabled me to become newly aware at the centre of my being that I was a member of Christ, a child of God, an heir of heaven. Tom Smail has said that 'a Christian becomes charismatic – that is, enters the dynamic field of the Spirit's action – not when he speaks in tongues and prophesies, but when he confesses Lord and Father.'[4] I did in fact receive the gift of tongues, but what was fundamental to me was a new awareness of God. 'The Spirit himself is the primary gift of God to believers' and this new release of the Spirit in my life brought me a new realisation of Christ not only with me, but in me and a new recognition of just whose son I was.

With this new awareness of God came a new praise. 'The impulse of the Spirit evokes thanks and praise to the Father'.[5] As in Acts chapter 2 so in my own new pentecost, the work of the Spirit produced praise for the mighty acts of God. Even the most familiar of hymns took on a new meaning. I had said if I sang 'Praise my soul, the King of heaven' once more at a wedding I would go pop. And then at a wedding soon after, the truth and power of its phrases came home to me in a new way,

> ransomed, healed, restored, forgiven
> who like me his praise should sing?

I found in the gift of tongues a new freedom in praise and a new vehicle in prayer. I started to use this gift regularly in my daily prayers and have done so ever since. Cardinal Suenens has said, speaking in tongues is

> a breach in the 'reserve' we assume as a system of defense. It helps us cross a threshold and, in doing so, attain a new freedom in our surrender to God. In psychological terms we could say that it is the voice of the subconscious rising to God, finding a manner of praying which is analogous to other

expressions of our subconscious in dreams, laughter, tears, painting or dance. This prayer within the depths of our being heals at a profound yet often perceptible level hidden psychological wounds that impede the full development of our interior life.[6]

A particular collect in the Book of Common Prayer had always jarred: 'Grant that we to whom thou has given a hearty desire to pray . . .'. The prayer would stick in my mouth. A hearty desire? You must be joking. Yet through spiritual renewal I found that God had indeed given me a hearty desire to pray. Not that I have always found it easy, far from it. Praying in tongues has helped but it has not exempted me from the usual need for discipline and regularity, and I have known barrenness in prayer along with so many others. But the desire has been there and remains because I know in prayer I share in the mystery of God himself in a special way. The power of prayer is no empty phrase.

With this new desire for praise and prayer I found too a new love for the Scriptures. Without abandoning any of the helpful insights of biblical and historical criticism, I found time and again in the Bible God's living Word. Bible study took on a new relevance and reading the Bible and using it devotionally became and have remained at the heart of my daily prayer.

In a memorable address to the 1968 Assembly of the World Council of Churches at Uppsala, Metropolitan Ignatias of Latakia said:

> Without the Holy Spirit God is far away,
> Christ stays in the past,
> the Gospel is simply an organisation,
> authority a matter of propaganda,
> the liturgy is no more than an evolution,
> Christian loving a slave morality.
> But in the Holy Spirit
> the cosmos is resurrected and grows
> with the birth pangs of the Kingdom,

the Risen Christ is there,
the Gospel is the power of life,
the Church shows forth the life of the Trinity,
authority is a liberating science,
mission is a Pentecost,
the liturgy is both renewal and anticipation,
human action is deified.

Something of the excitement and vision of those words corresponded well to my own experience and understanding of the Christian life as I knew more of the renewing power of the Spirit.

And the effects in my ministry were obvious. People began to hear a new voice and encounter a new confidence. Good management and organisation were now infused with a new spiritual reality. Many of the regular members of the church were drawn to a deeper commitment. New families and individuals started attending services and meetings. The church grew in a significant way. People found new life and new meaning for their lives. Out of our weakness we found a new strength.

And a new love. Rosemary and I were the first to know this in our marriage. But we soon saw a new loving concern grow in the church. Karen back home from hospital became one of the first to share in the new advance the church was making. People offered each other and newcomers strong loving support. Some opened their homes in a new way. People began to share their needs and their joys in newly formed housegroups. They prayed for each other and healing became a common experience. The worship of the church developed a new atmosphere that mingled warmth with reverence. Love had come again.

In one of the statements issued after the 1988 Lambeth Conference the bishops said:

Whoever has been baptised, either as an infant or as an adult, has been marked by Christ for salvation. Each individual must at some point, however, personally respond to that salvation, make that grace their own in Jesus Christ. In some this happens at their baptism, or later at confirmation, and for others at some other definite time and place in their personal history. In yet others it is a slow and growing awareness of their identity as children of God saved by Jesus. In either case this response is the work of the Holy Spirit in our hearts.

That had been our experience and the experience of many at St Luke's. But we knew its implications were not just for the immediate future. They should affect the rest of our lives. For this work of the Holy Spirit in us should, as the Lambeth Fathers said,

lead us into growing obedience to our Lord. Sometimes it may be accompanied by signs and wonders such as the gift of tongues or physical healing. It will always be recognised as genuine by the fruits of the Spirit: qualities of Christian discipleship, such as love, joy, peace, gentleness, kindness, humility and long suffering.

And here was the challenge. The Holy Spirit is a moving Spirit, moving us on, always in obedience to our Lord. In every age the Spirit comes upon us in power and dwells within us in peace. It was the same Spirit Bishop Charles Gore, one of the founders of the Community of the Resurrection at Mirfield, had spoken of when he said, 'When I recite "I believe in the Holy Catholic Church" I mean "I believe in the Holy Spirit reviving the church" '. Yes this was 'the Lord, the giver of life' reviving the church today as he had done before, and as he would do tomorrow.

But that was the point. Being filled with the Spirit is not a once-for-all encounter with God but a continuous reality of openness and response. 'Be filled with the Spirit' in Ephesians 5:18 is a present imperative: 'go on and on being filled' is the force of it. Here is a daily openness, a daily response, more a

daily increase. But isn't that the essence of the prayer at the end
of the confirmation service in the Alternative Service Book?

> Defend, O Lord, your servants with your heavenly grace,
> that they may continue yours for ever,
> and daily increase in your Holy Spirit more and more,
> until they come to your everlasting kingdom. Amen.

'Daily increase in your Holy Spirit more and more'. That is
what God wants for us all.

Slowly we began to realise the full implications of what we
were discovering. The Spirit was beckoning us forward, beyond
the nice feelings and sweet atmosphere to a new holiness, a
new obedience and a new faithfulness, and that was costly.

There is a special danger affecting growing churches and
ministers who are seeing a real responsiveness to their work.
It is the danger of being self-centred all over again. Holding
onto the last blessing, rather than being open to the Spirit's
new impulse. Celebrating the recent advance, rather than preparing for the next one. So often I have found that today's
radicals are tomorrow's conservatives, harking back to the good
old days and resisting the new directions the Spirit is calling us
into.

Early on in our experience of renewal, on the way to conducting a funeral, I called in one day to pray at a church. The
church, St Matthias Burley, had provided rich encouragement
for me and our people at that time. Seeing a woman arranging
the flowers by the altar, I walked up to her and said, 'I praise
God for this place!' She smiled and answered, 'Just praise
God!' It was a simple reminder of the true centre of all life
and ministry and the need to keep God in one's full focus.

With that focus we realised quickly that renewal was not just
for the church, but for the world, for the whole of life. The
church began to see our involvement and commitment to the
local community in a new light. We began to realise too that
God sought to renew the whole of life and that meant the

whole of our lives, not just the parts we were willing to allow
him to renew.

Uncomfortable self-examinations took place. Many stum-
bled, some fell. It was one thing to clap one's hands and sing
'Alleluia'. It seemed another to open all one's life to God and
allow his searching Spirit freedom to touch and cleanse and
heal.

We wanted to hear God, to know his will. We had learnt,
as Donald Coggan said, 'Christians believe in a God who
speaks. Ours is not a silent God, a God who sits, sphinx-like,
looking out unblinking on a world in agony. God speaks
because he loves. Love always seeks to communicate'. But we
found great difficulty in discerning his will for us. We made
many mistakes, many times confusing our voice for his and
only learning slowly how best to test our perceptions and find
his will through them.

But as we made mistakes and learnt from them, we found
God teaching us something vitally important: the readiness to
admit mistakes quickly and heed the lesson of them. Before,
we had been so nervous in his service we had dared little and
risked nothing. Now God had given us a more adventurous
faith and an active trust. But we remained learners and would
continue to do so. We walk by faith, not by sight.

Through our growth and our failure – for there seemed as
many mistakes as successes, as many blunders as blessings –
we came to appreciate the true costliness of the simple prayer
'Come, Holy Spirit'.

We had been accustomed to sing with great enthusiasm the
song 'Spirit of the Living God'.

Spirit of the living God, fall afresh on me, (repeat)
Break me, melt me, mould me, fill me,
Spirit of the living God, fall afresh on me.

But Tom Lees from Post Green taught us to sing those words
with great care if we meant them seriously. The renewing Spirit
would break us where we needed breaking for his greater

fruitfulness in our lives, for a deeper obedience to his mission
for the renewal of the earth.

Bishop Michael Ramsey has said,

> It is a costly thing to invoke the Spirit, for the glory of
> Calvary was the cost of the Spirit's mission and is the cost
> of the Spirit's renewal. It is in the shadow of the cross that
> in any age of history Christians pray: Come, thou holy Para-
> clete.[7]

A few years ago now I was talking to a young priest early in
his ministry. I saw his commitment and his effectiveness. Yet
I knew there was so much more possible in him. His ministry
I believed was very much his own creation, held within his own
power and control. I had seen times when he had opened
himself more deeply to the Spirit of God and been richly used
when he had done so. But then he had closed up again, and
returned to the familiar and tried and tested ways.

As we talked, I said to him, 'Don't be afraid of God'. I knew
there was so much more God could do in him and through him
if only he were willing to be truly open in costly surrender.

Of course it is costly and that is why he held back. To pray
'Come, Holy Spirit' is always costly. But it takes us to the
deepest reality and for the Christian it is the only true way
forward for personal life and ministry.

There was a time in the ministry of Jesus when people stopped following him because they recognised the cost it involved.
Jesus turned to the twelve and asked, 'Do you also want to
leave?' Simon Peter spoke up for them all, 'Lord to whom shall
we go? Your words are words of eternal life' (John 6:67–8). It
would not be easy, but there was no other authentic path before
them. 'We believe and know that you are God's Holy One.'

For us it is the same. God always beckons us forward. The
prayer 'Come, Holy Spirit' is always the prayer of the true
follower of God's Holy One.

Maybe you have never experienced the release of the Spirit

this chapter has described. In your weakness and need 'ask and you will receive, that your joy may be full' (John 16:24 RSV).

Maybe you stand at the threshold of new work, new responsibility or are in the midst of an onerous task that weakens you. Look afresh for the strength and confidence the Spirit can give, 'Come, Holy Spirit'.

Or maybe like me you look for a deeper work of God in your life, in the *whole* of your life and in those parts too you are slowest to surrender to him. Even your ideas.

Bishop John V. Taylor has said: 'God the Spirit is the unceasing animator and communicator, the inexhaustible source of insight, awareness, recognition and response. He is the awakener, and that is how he works upon us.'[8]

What is the Spirit awakening you to now? What breakthrough is he inviting you to make? Come, thou Holy Spirit, come.

> Heal our wounds; our strength renew;
> on our dryness pour thy dew;
>   wash the stains of guilt away;
> bend the stubborn heart and will;
> melt the frozen, warm the chill;
>   guide the steps that go astray.

The open church

The deaconess was really getting into her subject. She was explaining what it meant for the church to be the body of Christ. 'Now I want to show you what it means in practice.' The conference participants shifted uneasily on their seats. 'Please turn to the person next to you . . .' David Watson did so. Sitting next to him was an extremely attractive young woman he'd never met before. 'Turn to the person next to you and say to them, "I can't live without you" ' . . .

But that is what being the Body of Christ implies, mutual interdependence. 'We are the Body of Christ', the priest says in the Eucharist from the Alternative Service Book. 'In the one Spirit we were all baptised into one body. Let us then pursue all that makes for peace and builds up our common life'. Yet so often the reality is very different from the words. In some congregations we come together it seems, not to share anything but to bounce off one another like snooker balls. The common life doesn't seem to exist.

Yet that is what we are called to share in the life of the church and in the local congregation. St Paul affirms, 'Christ is like a single body with its many limbs and organs, which, many as they are, together make up one body' (1 Cor. 12:2). The implications are obvious, 'Just as in a single human body there are many limbs and organs, all with different functions, so we who are united with Christ, though many, form one body, and belong to one another as its limbs and organs' (Rom. 12:4,5).

There has been much discussion about the background to St Paul's description of the church as the Body of Christ. Stoicism,

the Hebrew concept of corporate personality and Jewish rab-
binical speculation about the body of Adam have all been
attested to. Bishop Michael Ramsey commenting on this has
said:

> It is one thing to ask what linguistic associations may have
> suggested the language to St Paul and another thing to ask
> what events or experiences would cause him to seek such
> vocabulary at all. Here we can say without hesitation that
> the cause was the power of the risen Christ so working
> through the Holy Spirit as to mould the lives of the Christians
> into being the medium of his own activity, the 'body' of his
> risen life.[1]

When St Paul encounters Christ on the road to Damascus
there is a recognition that he had already encountered him –
in his followers. 'Tell me, Lord,' Paul said, 'who are you?' The
voice answered, 'I am Jesus whom you are persecuting' (Acts
9:5).

For Paul to describe the church as the Body of Christ was
more than just a helpful illustration. It said something fundamental about the relationship of the church to Christ and his
embodiment in its life.

And the implications are obvious. St Theresa's famous words
spell out its significance for our service of others:

> Christ has
> No body now on earth but yours,
> No hands but yours:
> No feet but yours;
> Yours are the eyes
> Through which is to look out
> Christ's compassion to the world;
> Yours are the feet
> With which He is to go about
> Doing good;

Yours are the hands
With which He is to bless us now.

The work of the church in practice so often stands or falls
by how clearly or not Christ is seen in our lives and through
our loving service of others.

But St Paul applied the image of the Body of Christ first to
the relationship of Christians to Christ and each other. He
taught that Christ was the head of the body and that each of
us has to live in relationship to him. 'He is the first-born Son,
who was raised from death, in order that he alone might have
the first place in all things' (Col. 1:18 GNB). But under Christ
and in Christ our relationships to each other are of critical
importance.

A body is not a single organ, but many. Suppose the foot
were to say, 'Because I am not a hand, I do not belong to
the body,' it belongs to the body none the less. Suppose the
ear were to say, 'Because I am not an eye, I do not belong
to the body,' it still belongs to the body. If the body were
all eye, how could it hear? If the body were all ear, how
could it smell? But, in fact, God appointed each limb and
organ to its own place in the body as he chose. (1 Cor.
12:14–18)

St Paul was writing to the Christians in Corinth who were
strong on gifts, but short on love. If they are members of the
body of Christ, their mutual concern should be paramount.
Paul affirms, 'If one part suffers, all suffer together; if one
flourishes, all rejoice together' (1 Cor. 12:26).

For most of us I believe the reality of life in the local church
is very different from the picture Paul paints. Among many
clergy and ministers I find gifts are valued more than love. It
is more of a compliment to say of a fellow-minister, 'he is very
able' than to say 'he is very loving'. Churches which have
rightly stressed the importance of discovering and developing
people's gifts – 'let us use the different gifts allotted to each of

us by God's grace' (Rom. 12:6) – so often find an atmosphere developing which becomes more gift conscious than love conscious.

But then the reality breaks through from time to time and we see the body of Christ functioning as it should, open, supportive, belonging.

Michelle Guinness describes such an occasion in a house Eucharist in a Yorkshire mining town,

As the bread and wine was passed from one to another I looked around the room. The children sat at their parents' feet, quiet for once. The spouses who had refused to come in to any other meeting, sat beside their wives and husbands, relaxed and at ease . . . To be one body was to be bound by a blood tie, more family than family. And this was one of those rare occasions when we know it was so. The Jew in me always participated in this moment with a sense of wonder, that those whose paths might never have crossed, who might once have had little in common, separated by race, culture and prejudice, now belonged to each other because of all that this act symbolised.[2]

Here the local church was living out in its Eucharist the call to 'share the common life' (Acts 2:42).

But how do we do so on a regular basis in our relationships with one another? How does the local congregation share the common life? In his book *The Open Church* Jürgen Moltmann says, 'Congregation is no longer the sum of all those who are registered as members on the church rolls. Congregation is rather a new kind of living together for human beings'. Then he spells this out in six marks of the local church.

Congregation is a new kind of living together for human beings that affirms

– that no one is alone with his or her problems
– that no one has to conceal his or her disabilities

- that there are not some who have the say and others who
  have nothing to say
- that neither the old nor the little ones are isolated
- that one bears the other even when it is unpleasant and
  there is no agreement, and
- that, finally, the one can also at times leave the other in
  peace when the other needs it.[3]

Moltmann speaks of the sharing of weakness and disability,
the sharing of power and position, the special concern for the
powerless, the mutual forebearance and with the necessary
warmth of relationship, the necessary space too. He immedi-
ately answers the question in anyone's mind, 'Does this open
congregation of acceptance exist? We would be in a terrible
situation if it stood before us only as a biblically based demand.
If we open our eyes, we can also experience it in the power of
the Spirit in our very midst'.[4]

I began to experience it myself when I opened my eyes to
my own need and began to share my weakness with others. It
was a simple enough situation and yet later one of those present
said, 'The most significant moment was when John first asked
for help.'

A small group of us had begun to meet weekly for Bible
study and prayer. The group was formed soon after Rosemary
and I had known a new release of the Spirit in our lives. That
particular evening when it came to the time for prayer, I shared
a difficult pastoral decision I had to take and asked for help.
It was very simple and yet very significant. For the 'pro-
fessional' was asking help of 'amateurs' or so it seemed. As I
shared the problem without breaking confidences, and my
inability to resolve it in my own mind, so I opened the door
for others to do the same. A deeper sharing became possible.

I've seen it happen many times since. It can happen in home
groups, in parish staff or leadership team meetings, in groups
of people involved in pastoral care or the healing ministry when
time is given to face their own needs as well as those of others.
The priest or minister has a crucial role to play so often to

enable such sharing to take place. In so many of our situations, sharing is seen as only for the weak. Yet we are all weak in one way or another. We do belong to one another, and, once shared, our weakness can become our mutual strength.

Adrian Plass learnt the same lesson in a different situation. Involved with his wife Bridget in a short nightly discussion programme on TVS called *Company* he asked himself:

> What right did two ordinary people have to talk about Christianity in front of thousands of viewers when so many others were better informed, and certainly more consistent in the way they lived out their faith? The answer was, of course, none at all, and in realising this we realised what our contribution should be. If we could manage to be honest and open about the things, good and bad, that happened to us, and resist the temptation to make excuses for God by papering over the cracks in our lives, then we might offer hope and reassurance to people whose lives were just as frayed at the edges.[5]

For us the sharing of weakness and disability led eventually to the sharing of power and position. As people began to open themselves and their needs more to each other and discover in a deeper way than before mutual support and help, so at the same time the church began to grow in a significant way. And with that growth the demands on the parish staff grew. Pastoral oversight of a growing congregation became increasingly difficult and demanding. There were more people, more problems, more decisions and the burdens of leadership grew.

I had begun to share particular problems on an occasional basis with others, but increasingly I saw the need to do so on a more regular footing and with the most appropriate group. The common sense advice of Jethro to his son-in-law Moses rang bells with me too.

> Moses took his seat to settle disputes among the people, and he was surrounded from morning to evening. At the sight of

all that he was doing for the people, Jethro . . . said to him,
'This is not the best way to do it. You will only wear yourself
out and wear out the people who are here. The task is too
heavy for you; you cannot do it alone.' (Exod. 18:13, 14, 17,
18)

For Moses Jethro suggested he chose 'capable, god-fearing,
honest and incorruptible men' to share his burdens with him.
My first leadership team consisted of clergy and churchwardens.
Later we had a larger team (men and women) approved by the
P.C.C. and finally twelve people (including the parish staff)
appointed by the P.C.C. as part of the diocesan Local Ministry
scheme. Throughout we were a group where not only my burdens were shared, but other people's, and other voices carried
more weight at times than mine. Though the form of the group
may vary – P.C.C. Standing Committee, eldership, leadership
team, enlarged staff meeting – I would seek to work with such
a group in whatever situation I faced in ministry.

But the danger of any such group is that it takes itself too
seriously. Leadership in the church is a serious calling but we
know that Jesus is the head of the Body and that includes the
local church. Such an understanding gives a necessary humility
to our efforts. I heard Graham Cray once say at a conference
of clergy and lay leaders, 'We need to lose control of our
churches . . .' he paused before completing his sentence, 'so
that Jesus can lead'. We need to let Jesus' will take us forward
rather than ride our own hobby horses.

And in seeking to follow the priorities of Jesus for his church,
we need to be humble in another sense too. In our discussions
and reflections as leaders we need to pay special heed to those
whose concerns are so often marginalised in the church, as in
the world: the youngest and the eldest of our members.

The report of the Church of England's Board of Education,
'Children in the Way', challenged the church at every level to
see just where children were in its life. Rosemary was Bishop's
Adviser for Children's Work in the diocese of Ripon when the
report was published in 1987. The diocese covers parts of West

and North Yorkshire, both very urban and very rural. Rose-mary's work gave her a special awareness of just how much children are considered in the life of the church – and just how little. She saw much to encourage. But there was also much to sadden. At a P.C.C. meeting of a country parish one of its members stated that they did not want to encourage children to come to church, because that would mean changes and they were happy the way they were. In other situations Rosemary encountered similar attitudes, though rarely given such honest expression.

At my present parish of Manston, a large suburban parish in East Leeds, we reviewed our own work with children on Sundays. Now the whole church family gathers for the Euchar-ist at 9.30 a.m. before some of our younger members leave for part of the service for their own groups and activity. We're all together again, babies from the crèche too, for the Com-munion. A monthly family service was initiated, too, for fami-lies from outside the regular life of the church. We know children should be fully part of our congregational life.

The elderly too need to be fully included. When chronic sickness or disability makes attendance at church services and meetings more difficult or even impossible, it is vital that they are able to keep in touch with the rest of the body. At Manston with a long tradition of taking Communion to people's homes, we have extended that recently by the use of laypeople going out after the Sunday Eucharist. Though different churches will have different ways of handling it, any open church sharing the common life must ensure that 'neither the old or the little ones are isolated'.

Sharing weakness or disability among us, sharing power and position and having a special care for the most powerless in our community, we have been discovering some of the practical realities of common life in the body of Christ. But some of the most difficult lessons we have been most resistant to learning. Like bearing each other when there is no agreement.

There have been times when disagreement could be over-come when we faced what was happening in our lives. I remem-

ber one leadership team meeting at St Luke's. We were discuss-
ing what seemed a simple and straightforward issue, yet after
forty-five minutes we were no further forward. I felt some
people had been bringing personal unwritten agendas into their
reactions in the discussions. I interjected and asked each of the
twelve in the group to consider whether we were allowing any
of the problems of the day or anything else from our personal
lives to affect the discussion. We paused for a moment of quiet
reflection. Then two members of the team spoke up. One
admitted to having had a terrible day and only coming to the
meeting with great reluctance. The other said they were feeling
negative towards another person and that was affecting them.
A new atmosphere was established. People's problems and
needs were faced, and discussion proceeded well. Good
relationships are the best context for fruitful discussion and
decision.

But sometimes agreement won't come because of genuinely
held points of view that are irreconcilable. The Church of
England faces this on the large scale with the debate about the
ordination of women to the priesthood. But the local church –
in church council, leadership team or whatever – often faces a
deep division of view which somehow has to be borne in love.
We need to avoid pigeon-holing and labelling people and rush-
ing to take sides. 'We' are always more enlightened than 'them'
whoever 'they' are. I believe in praying and working for consen-
sus – the *homothoudion* ('of one mind') we encounter in Acts
4 when the early Christians prayed 'with one accord' (v. 24)
and were 'united in heart and soul' (v. 32). Sometimes that
degree of agreement cannot be found. In Acts chapter 6 we
read, 'as the number of disciples kept growing, there was a
quarrel between the Greek-speaking Jews and the native Jews'
(v.1 GNB). Growth can easily produce quarrels. That quarrel
led to a significant development in the life of the early church,
the appointment of seven deacons. Disagreements can be pro-
ductive for us, too, if we face them honestly and see what can
be learnt from them. Yet even if nothing positive emerges, we
need to bear with those we disagree with, make whatever

decision we have to and avoid a kind of ecclesiastical McCarthy-ism which seeks to banish the 'unenlightened'.

In writing of the church as the one body of Christ, St Paul spells out that we need to, 'Be humble always and gentle, and patient too, putting up with one another's failings in the spirit of love. Spare no effort to make fast with bonds of peace the unity which the Spirit gives' (Eph. 4:2, 3).

This care for unity and forbearance with one another needs to be expressed too in a church life which gives both warmth and space.

The need for warmth is obvious in the life of the local church. As Henri Nouwen has reminded us, 'One eye movement or one handshake can replace years of friendship when man is in agony. Love not only lasts forever, it needs only a second to come about'.[6] That deep and instant love should be the current flowing through the whole life of the church – expressed in our worship as well as our meetings.

I saw this strongly in a church I visited recently. There was a contagious warmth in the all-age congregation there. The Peace was shared in a natural and relaxed way and following a silence after Communion there was a time of open prayer when many joined in simply and easily and we knew the real presence of Christ in the Eucharist in every sense.

Yet the very strength of that gathering was also I think its weakness. The parish hall in which the congregation met was packed. When I entered it I felt a moment's apprehension. 'Will I find somewhere to sit?' The claustrophobic certainly would have found no place there. Though there was undoubted warmth, there was insufficient space.

The congregation's leaders knew the problem. The congregation had peaked, there was no room for new people or enquirers, a new larger church was being built. In our relationships too there is need for space as well as warmth.

The churchyard at Manston provides an attractive approach to the church. Through the lych-gate you walk down a path lined by six trees on either side – the twelve apostles. A beautiful idea. But flawed. Large branches from the trees started

falling and endangering those using the path – a local thorough-
fare as well as the church path. At first we wondered if the trees
were diseased. No, the tree surgeon diagnosed, just planted too
close to one another.

There needs to be spaces in our church's togetherness. Room
for the timid, the shy, those naturally less gregarious. Room
too for that part of all ourselves which at times needs solitude.
In his book *Life Together* Dietrich Bonhoeffer taught we can
only live together when we've learned the freedom to be alone.
The best families offer the warmth of belonging and the space
to grow. So should the church.

The church is called to be a healing community, of sharing
and openness, of tenderness and compassion, of warmth and
space. In the church we will 'rejoice with those who rejoice,
weep with those who weep' (Rom. 12:15). We will provide
hospitality, support, encouragement, reflection and silence. 'To
bind everything together and complete the whole, there must
be love' (Col. 3:14).

The priest's or minister's role in this is crucial. Positively or
negatively. Fr Nouwen writes of the aloofness that can be so
destructive.

> The tragedy of Christian ministry is that many who are in
> great need, many who seek an attentive ear, a word of
> support, a forgiving embrace, a firm hand, a tender smile,
> or even a stuttering confession of inability to do more, often
> find their ministers distant men who do not want to burn
> their fingers. They are unable or unwilling to express their
> feelings of affection, anger, hostility or sympathy. The para-
> dox indeed is that those who want to be for 'everyone' find
> themselves often unable to be close to anyone. When every-
> body becomes my 'neighbour' it is worth wondering whether
> anybody can really become my 'proximus' that is, the one
> who is most close to me.[7]

Sharing the common life must begin with those in ministry
and leadership. If we are to serve those who suffer, we must

recognise our own suffering. If we are to support the weak, we must acknowledge our own weakness. In practice churches so often reflect the clergy and ministers who serve them. Aloof clergy breed disconnected churches, where indifference is more evident than love. Sharing clergy willing to acknowledge their wounds as they seek to help in the healing of others breed wholesome churches, involved yet not intense, friendly but not pressuring, hospitable but not overbearing. There will be wounds unhealed, arguments unresolved but open and honest leadership will enable Christ to be known and shared among all who belong and he will be met too by those who come and see. For if the world cannot see Jesus in us how will it be able to see him at all?

There is an old legend in the Jewish Talmud about the coming of the Messiah. Rabbi Joshua Ben Levi came upon Elijah the prophet while he was standing at the entrance of Rabbi Simeron's cave. He asked Elijah, 'When will the Messiah come?'

Elijah replied, 'Go and ask him yourself.'

'Where is he?' asked Rabbi Joshua.

'Sitting at the gates of the city.'

'How shall I know him?'

Elijah spoke slowly in answer. 'He is sitting among the poor covered with wounds. The others unbind all their wounds at the same time and then bind them up again. But he unbinds one at a time and binds it up again, saying to himself, "Perhaps I shall be needed; if so I must always be ready so as not to delay for a moment".'

So Rabbi Joshua Ben Levi went to find the Messiah and he found him as Elijah said, sitting among the poor at the gates of the city. 'Peace be unto you, my master and teacher', he said to him.

'Peace be unto you, son of Levi', the Messiah answered.

'When is the master coming?' asked Rabbi Joshua.

'Today', he answered.

Rabbi Joshua returned to Elijah disappointed. Elijah asked him, 'What did he tell you?'

'He has deceived me. For he said, "Today I am coming" and he has not come.'

Elijah looked at him and said, 'This is what he told you. "Today if you would listen to his voice".'

What is the Lord saying to us today? If we are priests, ministers or laypeople called to positions of leadership in the church we need to know our own wounds, so that we may always be ready to help the healing of others. Whatever service we're called to render to others, let us recognise at first our own weakness and suffering and open ourselves not only to share but also to receive ministry from others.

If we are members of congregations, probably more disconnected than wholesome, where indifference is more evident than love, then we need to pray to be able to respond to the advice David Watson used to give, 'If you want more love in your church, give more love . . .' Ask for grace to serve and share – not only from your strength, but also from your weakness. As Fr Nouwen concludes:

A Christian community is a healing community not because wounds are cured and pains are alleviated, but because wounds and pains become openings or occasions for a new vision. Mutual confession then becomes a mutual deepening of hope, and sharing weakness becomes a reminder to one and all of the coming strength.[8]

9

Let the weak say 'I am strong'

He was there as he was everyday. A living picture of weakness and disability. Born a cripple he had no means of earning a livelihood. Except by begging. So each day he was carried to the same place and laid there – to beg. That way he survived, but it can hardly be said he lived.

Until those two men came. He asked them for money, as he asked everyone. But their response was different, 'Look at us.' The crippled man was all attention. 'I have no silver or gold, but what I have I give you: in the name of Jesus Christ of Nazareth, get up and walk.' And they helped him do just that. He went walking and leaping and praising God (Acts 3:1–10).

Peter and John, two of the first followers of Jesus, had no money to offer, but what they offered in the name of Jesus was healing and the transforming power to lead a new life. So often today's followers of Jesus in the western world seem well able to offer cash, but no transforming power. Silver and gold yes . . . but little else. Yet it is the power to change people, situations, even whole communities that is so desperately needed. The weak are going to the wall, and so often we seem powerless to help.

Graham and Gillian Burton went through the Church Missionary Society to Islamabad, the capital of Pakistan. Graham is now vicar of St Thomas' Church there and Gillian, a doctor, trains local health workers to take over the clinics she has helped establish. Graham says, 'I think one of the main things has been our encounter with poverty, trying to lay hold of the truth which is expressed in Scripture that God is the God of the powerless and he defends the orphans and the

95

fatherless and the widow.' Graham knows this means much more than charity. Involved in this is not so much giving to the poor, which basically we're quite good at, charity, but it is learning to advocate on behalf of the poor so that they, too, can receive their rights. So often these people, whatever society they're in, are denied their basic rights.[1] Supporting the weak, as St Paul bids us do, has practical implications for the poor and the powerless, wherever they are.

We realised that when we moved to the inner city. Of course it did not involve the depth of change or the degrees of poverty the Burtons encountered in Pakistan. I had already lived and worked in two parishes with large housing estates and predominantly working class communities. Yet in moving to Beeston Hill and Holbeck in South Leeds we were still encountering more widespread need and powerlessness than we had met before.

There was high unemployment, many elderly people living alone – the highest proportion of any community in Leeds – many single parents, a significant ethnic minority community of predominantly Asian origin and much poor housing stock, some of it due for demolition. Beneath the obvious needs of the area there was an ever present sense of powerlessness. People felt a lack of control over their lives and the conditions affecting them.

A good example of this when we first moved into the area was the tip. A piece of open land between Holbeck and Beeston known as Beggars Hill was being used for the dumping of council refuse. Eventually it was covered over by earth and reclaimed for the local community. But in our first summer there it was still being actively used. Refuse lorries delivered their loads every day.

We lived just two hundred yards from the tip and on hot days the smell was overwhelming. We had to keep our windows shut to prevent it from seeming to affect everything. And on windy days paper from the tip was blown into the surrounding streets giving the street cleaners a hopeless task.

I was appalled. But most local people I spoke to about it just shrugged their shoulders. 'There's nothing we can do.'

I knew this was on God's heart. That he cared for this community as much as for any other. Psalm 24 proclaims, 'To the Lord belong the earth and everything in it, the world and all its inhabitants', and I knew that meant for the people of Holbeck and Beeston Hill a quality of life that included clean streets and decent amenities. 'I know that the Lord will give to the needy their rights and justice to the downtrodden' (Ps. 140:12).

Some Christians have been slow to recognise the place social action plays in living out the gospel. Colin Marchant in his book *Signs in the City* suggests this test for any congregation.

> Ask for the first line of Psalm 23. Practically everyone will chorus 'The Lord is my Shepherd'. Ask for the first sentence of Psalm 24 and you'll get a silence before a single voice responds, 'The earth is the Lord's'. An exploration of why we know Psalm 23 but not Psalm 24 has to go beyond usage and sentiment; it must include the fact that personal faith sticks at that point. Full faith has to undergo three conversions: conversion to Jesus Christ, which is the fundamental, life-changing, inner transaction of faith; conversion to the Church as the body, fellowship and vehicle of the Gospel; conversion to the world as the created arena in which the Holy Spirit is forever working in the personalities, institutions and nations of humankind. To stop at the first is to stay forever in a truncated self-centredness; to remain at the second is to live within a spiritual ghetto; to hold all three together is the biblical way which is holistic and purposive.[2]

In the opening chapter of Mark's Gospel we read how 'Jesus came into Galilee proclaiming the gospel of God: "The time has arrived, the kingdom of God is upon you. Repent, and believe the gospel" ' (Mark 1:14–15). 'It was in the thought of the kingdom of his Father that Jesus lived and worked and died' as A. M. Hunter maintains.

The kingdom of God is absolutely central to the ministry of Jesus. But what is this kingdom that Jesus proclaims, inaugurates and looks forward to? Hans Kung has described it as 'creation healed' – the restoration of the whole of life to the original purpose of the Creator, a kingdom of 'justice, peace, and joy, inspired by the Holy Spirit' as St Paul described it (Rom. 14:17).

Jesus bids his followers to seek first God's kingdom. 'Set your mind on God's kingdom and his justice before everything else!' (Matt. 6:33) And living out that calling today as members of the body of Christ means, as Graham Cray has put it, 'working together in a fallen world, seeking to bring the forgiveness, healing and renewal of God's rule to bear on every area of life'.

'Thy kingdom come', we prayed, 'on earth as it is in heaven'. As I saw the implications of that for the whole life of the parish, I knew that action was needed in Beeston Hill and Holbeck and that the church had to become an instrument of change.

But first I needed to face my own weakness and discover in a deeper and fuller way the power of God's Spirit, before I could be used to help change anything. In effect I had to go into my own wilderness and there be renewed and equipped to tackle the tasks ahead.

It was the Spirit who led Jesus into the wilderness before leading him back to Galilee. In the wilderness Jesus faces temptation and is strengthened by the word and power of God. There he is equipped for the tasks that lie ahead. So St Luke is able to write, 'Jesus, armed with the power of the Spirit, returned to Galilee' (Luke 4:14).

And he comes to Nazareth, the place of his upbringing, his daily life and work. There in the synagogue he sets out his programme:

> The spirit of the Lord is upon me
> because he has anointed me;
> he has sent me to announce good news to the poor,

to proclaim release for prisoners
and recovery of sight for the blind;
to let the broken victims go free,
to proclaim the year of the Lord's favour.

(Luke 4:18–19)

The rest of the gospel is the working out of this programme.
Proclamation and practical action go together. The kingdom of
God is announced and demonstrated. Healing for the sick –
and liberation for the oppressed. The poor hear the good news
– and see it in action. Jesus' task is both an earthly one and a
heavenly one, as it is for his followers. The wholeness of the
gospel requires a whole response.

George Macleod, the founder of the modern Iona Community, loved to tell how

A boy threw a stone at the stained glass window of the
Incarnation. It nicked out the E in the word HIGHEST in
the text, 'GLORY TO GOD IN THE HIGHEST'. Thus, till
unfortunately it was mended, it read 'GLORY TO GOD IN
THE HIGH ST.'

At least the mended E might have been contrived on a
swivel so that in a high wind it would have been impossible
to see which way it read. Such is the genius and the offence
of the Christian revelation. Holiness, salvation, glory are all
come down to earth in Jesus Christ our Lord. The Word of
God cannot be dissociated from the Action of God. As the
blood courses through the body, so the spiritual is alone kept
healthy in its interaction in the High Street.[3]

Jane Galbraith sees that interaction in her own situation.
Writing from a hard-to-let council flat in Camberwell, South
London, she pens this hymn (which can be sung to the Slane
tune of 'Lord of all hopefulness').

Lord of our city, we bring you its pain,
The muggings, the dole queues, the lifts bust again.

The fear of each stranger and nowhere to play,
The waiting for buses at the start of the day.

Lord of the homeless, we bring you their cry,
The waiting on promises – pie in the sky –
The red tape and questions and sent on their way
The sense of frustration at the noon of the day.

Lord of all races, all colours of skin,
Please make us fight racism, help us begin
To see how our prejudice colours the way
We treat friends and neighbours at the end of the day.

Lord of our whole lives, we bring them to you,
We're powerless, defeated, 'til you make us new,
Then powered by your Spirit, we go on once more
With news of your wholeness, Good News for the poor.

In Beeston Hill and Holbeck it was the church school that taught us first how God can equip the powerless. Beeston Hill St Luke's Primary School was founded in 1873. It celebrated its centenary during the year I became the local vicar. The school did a terrific job – despite old and dilapidated buildings with outside toilets and small cramped playgrounds. One of my first tasks as vicar was to consider plans for the rebuilding of the school on a much better site nearby.

Then late in 1973 the government's axe fell – and we were taken out of the rebuilding programme. A public meeting was called. People may have felt powerless, but they were certainly angry. The school hall was crowded to hear the local education committee chairman try to explain the government's decision. Voices were raised in criticism of the government, the local council – and then someone criticised the school managers. That's when I stood up. As chairman of the school managers, I knew we were as frustrated as everyone else by the decision. So I started by saying that. And then without any notes or any clear sense where my speech was leading – I hadn't intended to speak before the meeting – I began to express my feelings on moving to the inner city. The tip, the unkempt streets, the feeling of being passed by, last in the line for everything – and now even the local school rebuilding programme had been stopped. 'We must unite,' I said, 'school managers, parents, teachers, church and local community. We must unite to fight the government decision and get it changed.' As I sat down there was a roar of approval from the meeting. Somehow in an innocent way I had struck a chord within people. I had articulated what many felt.

The local media helped our cause. Radio interviews, TV coverage – and best of all the *Yorkshire Evening Post* gave over its front page to our 'Scandal School' and most of page two as well. The new school campaign was truly launched! Petitions, letters, a candle of hope – and later through our MP Merlyn Rees a group of us, including the headteacher John Cooke, spent over an hour at the House of Commons with the Secretary for Education. Months passed, the campaign momentum was maintained, a general election and another government – more campaigning – and then the result we'd fought and prayed for. The school could be rebuilt! A fine new larger church primary school was created to serve the local neighbourhood in the name of Christ.

But the new-school campaign wasn't a one-off. People were recovering their confidence. 'They' could listen to 'us'. In 1975 work began on driving a four-lane motorway through the parish. When the plans had been published a few years before, only nine people had objected! When the work started and overnight streets were closed and local residents' and shop-keepers' lives disrupted, two hundred and fifty people crowded into another local school for a public meeting. I was asked to chair the meeting. It was too late to affect the building of the motorway – the opportunity for that had been missed. But the Holbeck Community Group was formed, action followed on other local issues and the Holbeck Gala was revived to cele-brate local community life. And the church which had wit-nessed other churches closing in the area in previous years had played a full part in the community's re-awakening and renewal, as it experienced renewal itself.

Bob Morris, my colleague and a gifted guitarist, wrote a song with a Calypso rhythm to celebrate what we had experienced.

> Motorway, motorway,
> You took our grass and trees away,
> You left us dust and mud and decay,
> Motorway, motorway.
> Motorway, motorway,
> We thought you'd drive us all away
> But we're still here and here to stay
> Growing in spite of you, motorway.
>> Jesus, Easter Man,
>> You rose from the dead and you come back again
>> Son of God, Son of Man,
>> You conquered death and you come back again.
>
> Scandal school, broken down
> They promised a replacement but they let us down.
> Till we marched down to London town
> We got our new school, the money was found.
>
> Churches close, faithful few,
> Keep on going less than one to a pew,
> But God shows us his word is true,
> Church grows again with life anew.

The last verse was a reminder of the inevitable struggle of life in the inner city.

> The night is dark, the road is long,
> But you send your Spirit to teach us your song,
> And we walk in the light of the Risen Son,
> Jesus, Easter Man.

In 1985 'Faith in the City' was published, the report of the Archbishop of Canterbury's Commission on Urban Priority

Areas. Subtitled 'A Call for Action by Church and Nation' it provoked much controversy. It was attacked by some politicians on frequently a misreading or partial reading of its proposals.

In its recommendations for the life of the church working in urban priority areas, I found it largely confirmed our own experience at St Luke's. 'How is the Church to take part in the history that the Spirit is making in our cities now?' it asked. And its answer was that, 'Churches in the UPAs have to become local, outward-looking and participating churches': *local* in their rootedness in the local community and commitment to it; *outward-looking* in putting mission first, in evangelism and service; *participating* in clergy and laity working together, using their varied skills, 'collaborating with the best expression of local life and . . . contributing to the transformation of life in UPAs through God's sustaining power and purpose!'[4]

But this missionary understanding of the church seeking to serve the kingdom of God seemed applicable outside Urban Priority Areas as well as within them. Five years of ministry in a suburban parish, though parts of it are in UPAs, have confirmed that conclusion. If we are to have a special concern for the weak and disadvantaged wherever we are, then certain principles of church life emerge. It is of a church life concerned first and foremost for the kingdom of God, seeking to bring the forgiveness, healing and renewal of God's rule to bear on every area of life.

Such a church will first be **sent** by the Spirit – Spirit led in its service, witness and work. It won't attend to every need – there are so many. It will seek to follow God's guidance as it establishes priorities for its work.

'The Spirit of God is the great missionary and only as he dominates the work and the workers can we hope for success'. John Mott's words of 1910 apply as much today. Without the express guidance and inspiration of the Spirit, our service will yield only weariness and frustration. We have seen it often enough in our own lives and ministry. Going round in ever

decreasing circles, achieving less and less. Tom Smail tells of
an occasion much earlier in his ministry when he was asked to
speak about the charismatic movement. But the person introdu-
cing him tripped over their tongue and said, 'Here is Mr Smail
to speak to us about the harassmatic movement'. Tom
responded by saying he had known well that movement in his
life and ministry already. It was the Holy Spirit that gave the
promise of becoming less harassed and more fruitful in God's
service.

Both our involvement in the new school campaign and the
formation of the Holbeck Community Group were products of
the Spirit's leading. We need first to wait on God and see him
order the agenda for the tasks we could work at. If we are
serving the kingdom, we need the priorities of the King.

Sometimes this can take a struggle to discover. With many
in the church catching a wider vision of God's purposes for
the whole community, eventually a member of the church's
leadership team at St Luke's was given the specific responsibility of heading up the social action. Several different projects
were looked at and eventually rejected, before at the right time
and through the right person the St Luke's Community Project
was born. It provided employment for some mentally handi-
capped people and others who had been out of work for a long
time, and it offered a number of services to the local community. For four years it made a significant contribution to
local people and the church's mission. But it was born in prayer
and the prompting of the Spirit.

Faced by the many needs within our communities, we need
to be sent by the Spirit – called, not driven – if our efforts are
to bear any fruit for the kingdom.

A sent church will also be a **serving** church – *being* good
news for the poor and powerless, wherever they are. Speaking
from his experience in South Africa Archbishop Desmond Tutu
has said:

The church must be ever ready to wash the disciples' feet, a
serving church, not a triumphalist church, biassed in favour

of the powerless, to be their voices, to be in solidarity with the poor and oppressed, the marginalised ones – yes, preaching the gospel of reconciliation, but working for justice first since there can never be real reconciliation without justice.[5]

The New School campaign showed me how the church could serve the disadvantaged, by sharing their struggles. In the suburban parish I'm in now, we've sought to do the same through an ecumenical Mission Audit. Anglicans, Methodists, Roman Catholics together have identified particular needs within the community of Cross Gates and working groups have been set up to tackle them. This was an easier task to start than to follow through, but in all the situations in which the church is set, God calls us to be good news for our neighbours.

Sent by the Spirit, serving the weak and disadvantaged, the church will also **speak up** for the kingdom, *bearing* the good news. This will involve both proclaiming the kingdom message and articulating the kingdom values. David Watson said, 'Evangelism and social action are the two blades of a pair of scissors; if we have one without the other, we lose our cutting edge'.

The task of proclamation is as urgent today as ever. In Eastern Europe Christians have played a significant role in the overthrow of Marxism. But what will replace it? A society alive to Christian faith and values – or full of undiluted Western materialism with pornography, sex shops and all the rest? Will the future be a new barbarism or a new synthesis of democratic freedom and revitalised Christianity?

A young East German in Central London two weeks after the Berlin Wall came down admitted, 'In the last fourteen days I have slept with several women, I have eaten all sorts of food and I've been drunk a number of times. If this is freedom, I don't want it!' Fortunately he was speaking to a Christian worker who was able to lead him to true freedom in Christ and a new life that would touch the depths of his being.

In Beeston Hill and Holbeck we found that speaking up for the weak and disadvantaged and sharing the good news of the gospel went hand in glove. One provided natural opportunities for the other. People were willing and interested in hearing about a God who cares when they saw something of his care in action.

But the Christian voice in some situations can be profoundly disturbing. A South American theologian commented, 'When as a Christian I give to the poor, they congratulate me for a Christian act. When as a Christian I ask why the poor are the poor, they accuse me of being a Communist.' If the gospel can comfort the disturbed, it can also disturb the comfortable. And that is true for our own churches and communities, as well as on the other side of the world.

Sent, serving, speaking up the church that seeks the kingdom will finally be one that **shows** the kingdom life, *revealing* the good news in its own life and relationships. Desmond Tutu has said:

> The church will demonstrate in its very life that Jesus has broken down the wall of partition and so in its common life there will be no artificial barriers to any Christian being able to participate fully.[6]

The Eucharist can focus this hospitality and openness. In the Peace, we share with one another. We encounter Christ in our neighbour, before we encounter him in the sacrament. 'Discerning the body' means recognising his real presence in each other as well as in the bread and wine (1 Cor. 11:27–30).

In Communion we gather together at the Lord's Table or feed from it. One family, of different ages, backgrounds, temperaments, occupations, social positions. Together we are empowered by the bread broken and the wine outpoured. The broken life of Jesus brings new life to us, weak as we are.

And in the Dismissal we are sent by the Lord for service: 'Send us out in the power of your Spirit to live and work to your praise and glory'. And the presence shared will be made available to all. As Gerard Hughes has said of the Eucharistic community,

As the presence of Christ becomes real in a congregation it will show itself in the openness of that congregation to all people, of all religions and none, of all races, nationalities and classes of society, but it will have a special care for those whom the rest of society overlooks and despises. In this way, the congregation really is living in the presence of Christ, in the power of his passion, death and resurrection.[7]

I recently went to a village church for the Eucharist. When I arrived five minutes before the service was due to begin, there were just eight or nine elderly people present. The organist was playing 'I'm building a people of power'.

It seemed absurd, but then, I reflected, so often the church seems like that. 'When you send forth your Spirit, you renew the face of the earth', Scripture maintains, but with a people like this? Surely a hopeless task.

It would have appeared no different in the earliest days of the church.

My friends, think what sort of people you are, whom God has called. Few of you are wise by any human standard, few powerful or of noble birth. Yet, to shame the wise, God has chosen what the world counts folly, and to shame what is strong, God has chosen what the world counts weakness. He has chosen things without rank or standing in the world, mere nothings, to overthrow the existing order.

(1 Cor. 1:26–8)

The weakness of the early Christians was no disqualification. Rather in their weakness, as 'mere nothings' God would use them to overthrow the existing order. The first three centuries after Christ revealed just that.

And for us today? 'The folly of God is wiser than human wisdom, and the weakness of God stronger than human strength' (1 Cor. 1:25). Time and again as we turn to God in our weakness he can use us beyond our imaginings for the renewal of his creation.

The psalmist reminds us:

No King is saved by a great army,
no warrior delivered by great strength.
No one can rely on his horse to save him,
nor for all its power can it be a means of escape.
The Lord's eyes are turned towards those who fear him,
towards those who hope for his unfailing love
to deliver them from death, and in famine to preserve them
    alive.

We have waited eagerly for the Lord;
he is our help and our shield.
In him our hearts are glad,
because we have trusted in his holy name.
Lord, let your unfailing love rest on us,
as we have put our hope in you.

(Ps. 33:16–22)

In our weakness, desiring to serve the weak, let us wait for
God and trust in his power to act. Let us be still before him.
Let us call upon him. Let us open ourselves to his love and
power. Then provided by the Spirit and prompted by him for
the tasks he lays before us, let the weak say 'I am strong' (Joel
3:10).

10

Still weak

Children have a special way of looking at things. A little girl screamed and came running in to her mother, 'There's a tiger in the garden!'

The mother jumped up and tore back the curtains. A St Bernard was wandering slowly across the lawn.

'That's not a tiger,' she said, 'that's Billy's dog from over the road. You know perfectly well it isn't a tiger. Go and ask God to forgive you for telling such a lie!'

Obediently, the little girl went upstairs. A few minutes later, she came down smiling.

'Well,' said her mother, 'did you ask God to forgive you for telling lies?'

'Yes,' she replied, 'and God said it was okay.'

'Okay?'

'Yes, God said the first time he saw Billy's dog he thought it was a tiger too!'

Jesus had a special love for children. He welcomed them and encouraged us adults to learn from them. In the openness, sense of wonder and joy in discovery so many children have, Jesus saw a lesson for us. 'He called a little child and had him stand among them. And he said: "I tell you the truth, unless you change and become like little children, you will never enter the kingdom of heaven" ' (Matt. 18:2–3 NIV).

Michel Quoist captures the message:

God says, I like youngsters, I want people to be like them.
I don't like old people unless they are still children.

I want only children in my kingdom, this has been decreed
   from the beginning of time.
Youngsters – twisted, humped, wrinkled, white-bearded –
   all kinds of youngsters, but youngsters.
There is no changing it, it has been decided, there is room
   for no one else.
I like them because they are still growing, they are still
   improving
They are on the road, they are on their way,
But with grown-ups there is nothing to expect any more.
They will no longer grow, no longer improve.
They have come to a full-stop.
It is disastrous – grown-ups think they have arrived.[1]

Christian living is a continuous process of adventure and
discovery. That's why we're called disciples (learners). We journey to God – with God. We can be confident of our destination
– nothing can separate us from his love in Christ – but we've
never arrived, in this life.

We never outgrow weakness here either. We never reach a
point when we can say, 'My weakness is behind me. I've
arrived!' We need to be always childlike, dependent on God's
grace and mercy.

We may and we do make progress in the Christian life.
Enduring that suffering, knowing that healing, handling that
stress, overcoming that sin, growing in prayer – but always
there will be weakness to acknowledge to ourselves, and to
God. Even for those we see as 'strong'.

Writing from his experience as chaplain of Lee Abbey, as
well as parish priest, David Runcorn has said:

It is one of the most frequent areas of neglect – the care for
the 'strong' in our churches. It is all too easy to assume that
because they are keeping going they must be all right.

Often the most tired, most isolated and discouraged were
not those who had experienced failure in their Christian lives.
Things had not gone especially wrong for them. They were

those whose strength had run out in the course of loving and faithful service.[2]

I recently had a period of sabbatical leave from my parish, in order to prepare and write this book. At the beginning of it for days I slept longer than I had done for ages. I was profoundly tired. The product of busy and richly blessed ministry. Yet draining and exhausting. 'Success' makes us weak, as well as 'failure'.

Faith is always, as Bishop Festo Kevingere said, 'Weakness hanging on to strength'. If we acknowledge our weakness, we can know his strength. Day by day, in the discipline of quietness and openness, we can find renewal for our lives in God's resources. 'Out of his infinite glory', Paul prayed for the Ephesians, 'may he give you the power through his Spirit for your hidden self to grow strong' (Eph. 3:16 JB). In our weakness we can grow strong through God's forgiveness, healing, compassion, power – through the unlimited resources of Father, Son and Holy Spirit.

I never cease to marvel at Mary's place in the story of our redemption. She was weak and vulnerable. Little more than a a young girl from an insignificant town called Nazareth, she was chosen by God to bear Jesus, the author of new life for us all. 'How can this be?' said Mary. 'I am still a virgin.' The angel answered, 'The Holy Spirit will come upon you, and the power of the Most High will overshadow you' (Luke 1:34–5). Ron Ferguson, the leader of the Iona Community, has said that Mary was 'the person who par excellence opened herself in lowliness to One who brings new life out of acknowledged impotence.'[3]

God can always bring new life for any who come to him, openly, honestly, receptively. We need to be open, for God never barges in through the closed door of our heart. We need to be honest, about our need, our sin, our pain, our fear, our failure or the weariness of our 'success'. We need to be receptive, for he is the life-giver, the one eternal personal source of love and power, joy and sensitivity, peace and purposefulness.

Then as we acknowledge our weakness before him, we can find his strength afresh.

When St Paul did so, he discovered that 'the power of Christ will come and rest upon me'. So he concluded, 'Hence I am well content for Christ's sake, with weakness, contempt, persecution, hardship and frustration; for when I am weak, then I am strong'. May we all discover that – and go on doing so.

Notes

Introduction

1 Desmond Tutu, *Who is God for us today?* (USPG), p. 7.
2 Robert Warren, *On the Anvil* (Highland), p. 29.
3 Gerard Hughes, *God of Surprises* (DLT), p. 123.

Chapter 1 Nothing to offer

1 Briege McKenna, *Miracles Do Happen* (Pan), p. 116.
2 Carlo Carretto, *Letters from the Desert* (DLT), p. 136.

Chapter 2 The wounded healer

1 Henri Nouwen, *The Wounded Healer* (Image), p. 72.
2 A. M. Ramsey, *God, Christ and the World* (SCM), p. 98.
3 Jürgen Moltmann, *The Open Church* (SCM), p. 103.
4 John V. Taylor, *Weep Not for Me* (World Council of Churches), p. 9.
5 William Temple, *Readings in St John's Gospel* (Macmillan), p. 178.
6 Peter Barnes, *Sunsets and Glories* (Methuen), p. 31.

Chapter 3 Facing suffering

1 Anthony Gardiner, *Confronting the Abyss* from St George's House, Windsor, Annual Review 1990, p. 31.
2 ibid. p. 33.
3 David Watson, *Fear No Evil* (Hodder and Stoughton), pp. 128–9.
4 Jürgen Moltmann, *The Crucified God* (SCM), pp. 273–4 quoting Elie Wiesel, *Night*.
5 John V. Taylor, *Weep Not for Me* (WCC), pp. 11–12.
6 Ray Moore, *Tomorrow is Too Late* (Penguin), p. 206.
7 ibid. pp. 206–7.

8   Ian Wilson, *The After Death Experience*, p. 207.
9   ibid. p. 208.
10 Gerard Hughes, *God of Surprises* (DLT), p. 134.

Chapter 4   *Hurt*

1   Garrison Keillor, *We are Still Married* (Faber and Faber), p. 365.
2   Paul Tournier, *The Healing of Persons* (Harper and Row), pp. 236–7.

Chapter 5   *Stressed*

1   Marjory Foyle, *Honourably Wounded* (Marc Europe), p. 14.
2   ibid. p. 15.
3   ibid. p. 16.
4   Gerard Hughes, *God of Surprises* (DLT), p. 101.
5   ibid. p. 101.
6   Robert Warren, *On the Anvil* (Highland), p. 172.
7   John A. Sanford, *Ministry Burnout* (Paulist), p. 23.

Chapter 6   *The buck stops here!*

1   Laurens van der Post, *The Night of the New Moon* (Penguin), p. 122.
2   John V. Taylor, *A Matter of Life and Death* (SCM), p. 30.
3   C. S. Lewis, *Surprised by Joy* (Fount), p. 179.
4   Michel Quoist, *Prayers of Life* (Gill and Macmillan), pp. 101–2.
5   Told in Cardinal Suenens, *Open the Frontiers* (DLT), p. 40.
6   Marjory Foyle, *Honourably Wounded* (Marc Europe), p. 129.
7   Laurens van der Post, *The Night of the New Moon* (Penguin), p. 30.

Chapter 7   *Breakthrough*

1   Quoted by Cardinal Suenens, *A New Pentecost?* (DLT), p. 73.
2   Cardinal Suenens, *A New Pentecost?* (DLT), p. 74.
3. ibid. pp. 217–223.
4   Tom Smail, *The Giving Gift* (Hodder and Stoughton), p. 13.
5   A. M. Ramsey, *Holy Spirit* (SPCK), p. 28.
6   Cardinal Suenens, *A New Pentecost?* (DLT), pp. 102–3.
7   A. M. Ramsey, *Holy Spirit* (SPCK), p. 131.
8   John V. Taylor, *A Matter of Life and Death* (SCM), p. 8.

Chapter 8   The open church

1 A. M. Ramsey, *Holy Spirit* (SPCK), pp. 76–7.
2 Michelle Guinness, *Promised Land* (Hodder and Stoughton), p. 109.
3 Jürgen Moltmann, *The Open Church* (SCM), p. 33.
4 ibid.
5 Adrian Plass, *The Growing Up Pains of Adrian Plass* (Marshall Pickering), p. 61.
6 Henri Nouwen, *The Wounded Healer* (Image), p. 67.
7 ibid. p. 71.
8 ibid. p. 94.

Chapter 9   Let the weak say 'I am strong'

1 From the C.M.S. Presentation 'Our Strength is Weakness'.
2 Colin Marchant, *Signs in the City* (Hodder and Stoughton), pp. 112–3.
3 Quoted in Ron Ferguson, *Chasing the Wild Goose* (Fount), p. 86.
4 'Faith in the City' (Church House), p. 77.
5 Desmond Tutu at Pretoria University, March 1981. Quoted in Simon Lee and Peter Stanford, *Believing Bishops* (Faber and Faber), p. 173.
6 ibid. p. 173.
7 Gerard Hughes, *God of Surprises* (DLT), pp. 132–3.

Chapter 10   Still weak

1 Michel Quoist, *Prayers of Life* (Gill and Macmillan), p. 3.
2 David Runcorn, *Space for God* (Daybreak), p. 40.
3 Ron Ferguson, *Chasing the Wild Goose* (Fount), p. 193.